WHAT PEOPLE ARE SAYING ABOUT
STANDING STRONG IN THE STORM

Every leader experiences storms. Therefore, the question isn't if you'll encounter rough waters but what you'll do in the midst of those trials. Greg Davis has penned an authentic and powerful account of his family's journey—it will inspire, affirm, and challenge you.

—Sam Chand
Leadership Consultant and Author of *Leadership Pain*

Greg Davis's new book is a powerful departure from the flood of smug, saccharine pronouncements that God's people will never endure storms—but it is not gloomy and hopeless. I recommend *Standing Strong in the Storm* because this redemptive mixture of tough reality and triumphant faith is an important read for modern believers.

—Dr. Mark Rutland
Executive Director of the National Institute of Christian Leadership

Greg Davis is well-acquainted with navigating adversity. His new book, *Standing Strong in the Storm*, is an inspiring and encouraging guidebook on how you, too, can face the storms of life and come out victorious on the other side.

—Todd Starnes
Author and Nationally Syndicated Radio Host

Leaders will experience unexpected storms that put their leadership resiliency to the test. The good news is that God does not expect us to go through them alone. He promised to walk with us "through the valley of the shadow of death." Greg Davis draws from his personal experiences and powerful scriptural principles to help you stand strong in your storm.

—Doug Clay
General Superintendent of the Assemblies of God

I have known Greg Davis for many years. *Standing Strong in the Storm* is a treasure trove of fresh insights from God's Word and a valuable resource to empower people to thrive in times of trouble. This book is written in a manner that will help you *experience* the truths of the Bible instead of just reading them.

—Dr. Ron McManus
Consultant and President, Legacy Transition Group

With all the setbacks we face in the world these days, we need more trusted voices who can speak to the realities of pain and suffering from a perspective of real hope. Greg Davis has been a lifelong friend. I'm overjoyed that you now get to experience for the first time what I have known for years. This is a book everyone should read.

—Reggie Dabbs
International Communicator, Pastor, Public School Speaker

Pastor Greg Davis delivers the straight truth about navigating the inevitable storms of life. That truth comes from a deep well of personal experience and the Scriptures. Everyone will face storms. We will not all face them grounded in faith-filled purpose. But we can. Greg Davis shows the way in *Standing Strong in the Storm*.

—Travis Johnson
Lead Pastor, Pathway Church
Executive Director, People for Care & Learning

It is rare to encounter a story as compelling or a storyteller as real as Greg Davis. Then again, it is rare to meet someone who has faced more adversity than Greg yet has come out on the other side still trusting and still hoping. This book doesn't just describe the darkness of difficulty; it reveals the relentlessness of God's gracious light that never stops pursuing us.

—John Driver
Writer, Minister, Coauthor of
*Not So Black and White: An Invitation to Honest
Conversations About Race and Faith*

Practical but powerful! Personal yet Biblical! While many pastors are experts in exegeting a text, Pastor Greg Davis is also an "expert example" of the text. I've been privileged to watch him over the past two decades grow a congregation while navigating an unimaginable number of personal storms in life. Now, on the other side of many of those storms, Pastor Davis shares spiritual insight into overcoming life's most difficult challenges. After the past couple of years of a worldwide pandemic storm, this book is a must-read for anyone who desires peace and victory. How do you maintain faith when times are so frustrating? Against the backdrop of Jesus walking on water during an intense storm, Pastor Davis's book offers hope and skills to all.

—Dr. Bartholomew Orr
Senior Pastor, Brown Missionary Baptist Church
Southaven, Mississippi

Epic Bible stories have a tendency to remain just that—"Epic"—without really informing, shaping, or defining our perspective of God and His power in our daily lives. In *Standing Strong in the Storm*, Greg Davis takes some of the most epic stories and encounters with Jesus and brings to light incredibly practical principles that can grow our faith in times of trouble.

It's one thing to write a book about principles that you've learned cognitively or experienced secondhand. However, I've known Greg and Nancy Davis for over 25 years, and I've watched from a distance the struggles described in this book. I can say without any hesitation that the principles outlined in *Standing Strong in the Storm* have been lived out in front of their congregation, family, and friends. I appreciate the vulnerability of Greg's personal story as well as the keen Biblical insight into the theology of suffering and perseverance—and I know you will too.

—Patrick Conrad
Lead Pastor, Compel Church
Desoto County, Mississippi

"Strength can only be increased by overcoming resistance!" It is my great joy to recommend *Standing Strong in the Storm,* written by my friend and mentor, Pastor Greg Davis. I pray that you will be stirred as you hear the cry and the passion of his heart to see a generation move from fear to faith. Each chapter will challenge you and inspire you to embrace every season in your life and to walk in the fullness of God›s destiny for you. As Pastor Greg takes you on his journey of overcoming his own personal storms to accepting and fulfilling the purpose of God in his life, I hope that you will take his practical wisdom and insight and apply it to your own storms—allowing a limitless God to transform your limitations into His masterpiece.

—Josh Wilbanks
Pastor, Author, and Evangelist

Greg Davis challenges us to look at the story of Jesus walking on water from a new perspective. This book will give you hope and strength to weather your storms—and to find victory in the midst of them!

—Martijn van Tilborgh
Strategic Marketing Architect and Consultant
Sanford, Florida

CULTIVATING RESILIENCE
IN TIMES OF TROUBLE

STANDING STRONG

IN THE

STORM

GREG DAVIS

ARROWS&
STONES

For foreign and subsidiary rights, contact the author.

Cover design by: Sara Young

Cover Photo by: Emily Shuff Photography

ISBN: 978-1-957369-52-5   1 2 3 4 5 6 7 8 9 10

Printed in the United States of America

This book is dedicated to my favorite people on the planet—Nancy, my amazing wife and sweetheart since second grade and our incredible children, Colton and Anna Grace! I am so proud of all of you for how you have persevered through so many life-threatening health issues over the years. Like the apostle Paul, you have fought the good fight and kept the faith *in the face of unimaginable adversity. And you have trusted the Lord and allowed Him to create in you a Christ-like character that inspires other people. As you know, words are my "thing,"—but they fall short in expressing how much I love and appreciate you.*

Contents

ACKNOWLEDGMENTS

Cornerstone Church—One of the most important principles I have learned is that we are not designed to navigate the storms of life alone. God has created human beings with a genuine need for fellowship, relationships, and mutual encouragement. Roughly 70 percent of the storms our family has faced have occurred while I have been pastoring Cornerstone Church in Southaven, Mississippi.

Cornerstone is an incredible family of believers that have prayed for us, supported us, and encouraged us in the good times and in times of trouble. It would be hard to imagine what it would have been like to endure such seasons of adversity without the collective strength of such a wonderful church. God has used Cornerstone to provide that same love and encouragement for thousands of people through the years.

Ron McManus—We all need mentors, and Ron McManus has been a significant mentor in my life for the past eleven years. He has helped me with church growth strategies but even more in the area of personal growth and development. His encouragement and advice helped to accelerate this book project at a time when it was not moving forward at an acceptable pace. He introduced me to the incredible team at Four Rivers Media, and that changed everything!

Four Rivers Media—Words fall short of expressing my appreciation to Martijn van Tilborgh and the other amazing people at Four Rivers Media. Within a few short days of my introduction, I was surrounded by an entire team of people who were intent on encouraging and advising me with the most effective strategies to get my first project published far sooner than I expected.

My deep appreciation goes to John Schondelmayer, Caroline Edwards, Matt Green, Debbie Chand, the design team and all the other wonderful people at Four Rivers Media.

CHAPTER 1

WISHING FOR A NIGHTMARE

I was startled and awakened by a clap of thunder that sounded like it was right on top of me! The first sensation I can remember was the huge raindrops pelting my back through the heavy quilt my father had thrown over me as he carried me towards the entrance to the storm cellar in the backyard. My dad flung open the storm cellar door, and my mom, who was carrying my three-year-old brother, made her way down into the shelter. The next sound I heard was my mother's voice crying out for help. She had slipped and fallen down the steps.

The storm shelter had not been properly sealed, and almost two feet of water had seeped in. Fortunately, the water cushioned my mom's fall and prevented any injury to her or my brother. With the shelter flooded, we hurried back into the house to ride out the storm. The memory of this chaotic event was seared into my eight-year-old brain and remains firmly embedded to this day. My childhood was dotted with memories of storms that prompted my family to seek shelter.

Most people have a storm story to tell; some are tragic—others, not so much. Storms have held a certain fascination for people since the beginning. Watching the elements of nature collide in combat over the landscape produces feelings of awe as we witness such power. Storms also remind us that there is much about life over which we have no control. The word "storm" is defined as "a violent disturbance in [the normal conditions of] the atmosphere."[1] This is why storm is used in a figurative sense to describe unexpected disturbances in the normal conditions of our lives. These *disturbances* or times of crisis can come in many different forms. And they can cause serious problems in our physical health, our family relationships, our careers, our finances, and—many times—our mental, emotional and spiritual well-being.

We all experience storms in life, and the main focus of this book is to encourage and equip people to persevere through seasons of adversity and come out stronger on the other side. The story above alludes to one of my earliest experiences with a weather-related storm. Fast-forward twenty years, and I found myself facing another type of storm that I couldn't control. This time, it would be the first of many that were to follow.

WHEN THE STORM STRIKES

I woke up on my 29th birthday on a typically uncomfortable hospital room couch. At that moment, I realized that everything I had hoped was just an awful nightmare was, in fact, reality. About twenty-four hours earlier, my wife, Nancy, and I had experienced the most thrilling moment of our lives. After eight years of praying and waiting, our battle with infertility ended with the birth of our son, Colton. The ecstasy of finally being able to hold our firstborn was indescribable. Life was perfect! And it stayed that way—for about two hours.

---

1 "The Oxford Pocket Dictionary of Current English," *Encyclopedia,* 21 Jun. 2022, https://www.encyclopedia.com/earth-and-environment/atmosphere-and-weather/weather-and-climate-terms-and-concepts/storm.

Colton was taken to the nursery to allow Nancy some time to rest and recover from the labor and C-section. After a couple of hours, I went down the hall to the nursery to bring him back to our room, only to find that he was not there! I kept looking through the window, trying to read the name tags on the little clear bassinets, but none of them had his name attached. Confused, I started tapping on the window to get the attention of one of the nurses. She came out, and when I asked where Colton was, she said, "Hasn't anyone notified you?" I said, "Notified me about what? Where is my son?" That's when she informed me that Colton had been rushed to the neonatal intensive care unit. When I asked why, she said the doctors would have to explain.

As I hurried downstairs, my mind raced with questions, and fear began to fill my heart. My first glimpse of Colton in the NICU is seared into my memory. He was lying in a hospital bassinet connected to life support by a mass of wires and tubes. When I asked his nurse what was wrong, her answer felt like a punch in my stomach. "I'm so sorry, but it is evident that your son has been born with significant heart defects. He will definitely need heart surgery and possibly a heart transplant."

> ## After all the years of praying and waiting, how could this be possible?

I could not believe what I was hearing. After all the years of praying and waiting, how could this be possible? I kept thinking that there must be some mistake. I was informed that an urgent call had been placed to a pediatric cardiologist who was on his way to examine Colton. Within the next few hours, he would be transported to Le Bonheur Children's Hospital. At this point, my memory becomes a bit hazy, probably because I was in a daze of devastation. I remember shuffling out into the hallway, leaning back against the yellow subway-tiled walls and sliding down onto the floor in a pool of tears, despair, and disbelief.

I don't really remember how long I sat there, but at some point, I gathered myself enough to realize that I had to go drop this bombshell on my wife. I made my way back up to the room and began to try to relay the information. But I couldn't. I'm not exactly sure what was happening to me at that point, but I literally could not speak. I remember trying to form the words, but they wouldn't come out. The words were there in my mind, but when I tried to speak them, what came out was unintelligible. I would try to talk, realize that I wasn't making any sense, shake my head, and then try again.

Nancy was already crying even though she didn't know exactly why. She knew that I had learned something that had devastated me so completely that I had lost the ability to do what I do best—communicate. I don't know if I was on the verge of a mental/emotional breakdown, but it was at least five minutes before I regained enough control of myself to convey what I had been told. Our perfect world had been shattered in less than two hours, and along with it, our vision of the future. We cried and prayed with each other and with our family that had gathered for this momentous day—not knowing just how momentous it would turn out to be.

A SPIRITUAL STORM

This early in the process, we were still in shock and denial that it could even be happening. How could God allow this? Was it not enough that we had struggled so long to even conceive a child, and now this? It was at that point that the spiritual warfare aspect of our situation intensified. It began with a memory of something that had happened before I even knew there was a problem. It started when I had approached the viewing window of the nursery to bring Colton back to the room.

As I walked up to the window, I noticed a man standing there, smiling wide and beaming with pride as he gazed through the glass at his healthy newborn son. Then I noticed something. The air around this man carried the distinct odor of marijuana—fresh. He had no doubt been smoking pot sometime that morning either before, during, or after his son's birth. The devil began to whisper in my ear, *This is what you get for serving God? You have answered the call to ministry and devoted your life to serving God and others, and your son is going to die! This man doesn't serve your God, and his son is healthy!*

I knew immediately that these thoughts were an attack of the enemy, but in my mind and emotions, the questions seemed valid. Why would God allow this to happen? No doubt, as you are reading this part of our story, you remember times in your own life when you've had similar questions. We all experience things in life that don't make sense to us and tempt us to ask why. As our story unfolds, you will have the opportunity to examine your own unanswered questions and develop a strategy to deal with them in an effective and healthy way.

Later that afternoon, the pediatric cardiologist came into our room and gave us a report. He informed us that Colton had been born not just with one but with multiple life-threatening heart defects. The combination of defects meant that this would not be a one-time surgical procedure or a simple repair. The worst case scenario was that our son would not survive. One of the nurses had indicated that she was hopeful that Colton would survive being transported by ambulance to the local children's hospital. I guess she was trying to be encouraging, but the fact that his short-term survival was even in question was the exclamation point on an already devastating day.

According to the doctors, the best-case scenario might possibly allow Colton to grow into adulthood. But at that point, the prognosis for a normal life seemed unlikely. In any case, Colton would have to endure multiple heart surgeries and numerous other heart-related procedures. We were told that he would undergo his first heart surgery just a few days later. It would not correct his issues, but it would hopefully keep him alive long enough to undergo a much more complex surgical correction about a year later.

Our minds were swirling with questions that any parent would have in this circumstance. *If Colton survives, what will be his quality of life? Is it possible for him to have a normal life span? What about being active and having a normal lifestyle?* Of course, the doctors let us know that it was too early to accurately answer these questions, but the general prognosis they gave was less than encouraging. A dark cloud enveloped my mind, and the enemy of my soul began, once again, to whisper in my ear: *The happy future you envisioned is gone. Get used to it because the darkness and despair that you are drowning in right now is your new normal. Your God has failed you!*

> Deep down, I wondered if all the joy had just been sucked out of our future.

I knew this was the voice of Satan, and I knew it was spiritual warfare. But deep down, I did wonder if all the joy had just been sucked out of our future. It was hard to imagine ever laughing again, and for those who know me, life without laughter would be like hell on earth. Would there actually be good days ahead for our family? In the emotional darkness of that time, any positive expectation or hope for the future seemed to be slipping away.

A WORD FROM GOD

In those moments, just after I woke up on my birthday and realized that the previous twenty-four hours were not just a nightmare, I did the only thing I knew to do. I poured my heart out to the Lord in prayer quietly, so I wouldn't disturb Nancy who had finally drifted off to sleep after the emotional hurricane of Colton's birth day. As I reached for my Bible, it fell open to Psalm 9:1. I am typically not a "pick and poke" Bible verse person, but this time was definitely God-directed. Study of the ancient Hebrew reveals that Psalm 9 is a psalm of David written to the tune of "The Death of a Son." The first line of the psalm says, "I will praise you, O Lord, with my whole heart" (NKJV). That's when it happened.

The Holy Spirit's voice came piercing through the darkness of that hour like a lightning bolt, and I heard God speaking in my spirit, *Your son will stand in my presence and praise me with a "whole" heart.* At that moment, I knew that Colton's heart would be made whole. The darkness lifted, and somehow, I felt assured that no matter what we had to face in the future, Colton was going to be alright! This was one of many times in our lives that we have experienced the tangible sense of what Philippians 4:7 describes as "peace that surpasses all understanding" (author paraphrase). This basically refers to a supernatural peace from God that doesn't make any sense—in light of our circumstances. As I look back to those moments of prayer and seeking the Lord, my heart is filled with gratitude for the overwhelming sense of peace that God imparted to me through his Word. I don't know how we would have survived without that word from the Lord in the middle of the worst storm we had ever faced—up to that time.

A CHALLENGING PATH

Colton was transported to the local children's hospital and underwent his first heart surgery when he was seven days old. He spent the first three weeks of his life in the hospital—mostly in the ICU. So, our initiation as parents was spent in a fog of emotion and a flurry of beeps, bells, and alarms from all the machines that were keeping Colton alive and stable until his tiny little body could recover from all the trauma and stress of the surgery. Then, the day finally came when we celebrated the miraculous privilege of bringing our son home for the first time!

It was a day of great celebration mixed with a measure of anxiety. Most new parents experience a bit of apprehension at the realization that this new little life is 100 percent dependent on them for survival. The weight of that realization was heavier for us because of Colton's condition. At first, we were terrified that we might make some kind of a rookie mistake that would harm him in some way. But as the days passed, we settled into our new life as parents and relished every moment with our little miracle boy.

The next sixteen months were relatively normal for our family although we knew that the first surgery was actually a provisional procedure that was intended only to buy him some time so that he could grow and become stronger. Therefore, when I say those months were relatively normal, I mean the day-to-day routine was fairly normal with the exception that every moment of that time, we knew another more complex and dangerous surgery was in our future. We had been informed that the target time for that surgery would be sometime before Colton reached his second birthday. Even with his issues, he grew and thrived in his first year of life. And we lived each day in the confirmation that all the things that Satan had whispered in my ear the day that Colton was born were lies. Our lives were filled with joy and laughter as we watched our little boy grow.

A RIVER OF QUESTIONS

The time for his next surgery came when he was just seventeen months old. That operation was an extremely complex and relatively new procedure that had been developed to address the unique combination of issues in Colton's heart. Any parent who has ever had to watch their child be wheeled away into surgery knows the torrent of emotions that comes in that moment. You basically stand there feeling totally helpless to alleviate the suffering and pain that you know your child is going to experience. Questions flow like a raging river: *Why? Why does my innocent little child have to endure this pain while other children are spared? Did I do something to cause this? Am I being punished somehow? How could God allow this? What possible purpose could this suffering serve?* The questions are endless, and the answers are often elusive. But deep down, we knew that we didn't do anything to cause Colton's heart defects.

Our faith answered some of the questions, and logic answered others. But the fact is that anyone who goes through times like this will be faced with a choice of how to live with all the questions that remain *unanswered*. At the end of all the emotional turmoil and mental gymnastics, you basically find yourself with two choices—get stuck in your unanswered questions, or move forward in spite of them. The option to quit can be very tempting when you can't understand why God would allow all of this pain and suffering in your life. Many times, we have found ourselves at that crossroads of temptation to give up and afterwards to deal with feelings of guilt over the doubts that we battled.

Through it all, I have come to believe that the greatest expression of faith in God is to keep moving forward when you can't comprehend the path you're walking. In those days, I made up my mind that when I don't understand—I'll still stand! We can get bitter, or we can get better. Nothing good ever comes from choosing the former. Though we didn't fully understand it back then, we would be forced to choose between those pathways many more times. Colton's second heart surgery was extremely complex, but it was successful and allowed him to grow and develop normally. He was able to be active, play sports, and just enjoy being a little boy.

> One of the greatest expressions of faith in God is to keep moving forward when you don't understand the path you're walking.

The day of Colton's birth marked the beginning of a season of storms in our family that we never could have imagined. Every member of my family has faced life-threatening battles with deadly diseases. So many times, we have stood in shock and disbelief as each new health hurricane roared across the landscape of our lives. During the darkest days and most challenging times, our main focus was to just try to make it through the day. I will elaborate further on the details in later chapters, but for now, let's focus on some universal truths.

No one's life is stormproof! Everyone faces adversity. *The storms of life can either lead to our destruction or to our destiny.* The deciding factor in how a crisis will ultimately impact us lies in how we choose to respond to our storm. Our experiences taught us that *it's all in the WRIST*—What Response I Select Today. There are many valuable lessons that can be gleaned in the darkest days of our lives, but only if we respond correctly to times of testing. We would never have survived without the Word of God. I related earlier how, on the morning after Colton's birth, the Lord pierced through the darkness of those moments with the blinding light of His Word. In an instant—*nothing changed, and everything changed.* Nothing changed in Colton's condition, but everything changed in my expectation.

> In an instant—nothing changed,
> and everything changed.

As time passed and new attacks on our family's health were launched, God was faithful each time to give us exactly what we needed to encourage us and equip us to persevere. Many times in the New Testament, we witness Jesus using earthly illustrations to help people understand heavenly truth. This book will take us on a journey through some of the *storm stories* in the Bible. Our goal will be to examine accounts of how God's people experienced actual physical storms so that we can identify kingdom principles to help us navigate times of trouble. The pathway that our family has walked has given us a passion to encourage and equip people with the Word of God and inspire them to never give up—no matter what!

CHAPTER 2

IT'S TIME TO CROSS OVER

Colton's story accounts for just a fraction of the storms that our family has endured. I will share more later in the book. But the things that we have experienced have given us a deep compassion for people who are struggling to survive the worst times of their lives. Our desire is to share the foundational principles from God's Word that have enabled us to successfully navigate our darkest days.

> If you respond correctly to your storm,
> God can transform the pain of misery
> into the power of ministry.

If you respond correctly to your storm, God can transform the pain of misery into the power of ministry. The things that the enemy of your soul uses to try to destroy you can become weapons of warfare in your hands. Once you have successfully navigated your storm, you are equipped to help others who are going through similar circumstances. There is a powerful thought in 2 Corinthians 1:4. It basically says that God comforts us through all of our troubles, so that we can comfort others who are in trouble with the same comfort that God has given to us. Helping people navigate the most difficult times of their lives is one of the main purposes of this book.

There are many stories in the Scriptures that describe actual physical storms that people experienced. Within those narratives, there are powerful principles that can equip us to thrive in the difficult days of life. In the next few chapters, we will zoom in on a well-known story in the New Testament. It is the story of a major storm that forever changed the lives of the disciples. But the impact of this event was not limited to that small group. God used that storm to help mold the character and faith of the disciples who, with the later addition of Paul, became the core group that literally changed the world by spreading the gospel.

From the modern-day era all the way back to the New Testament times, each new generation of believers has been influenced by the generation before them. So, in a very real sense, the impact of this storm is still being felt today! The story I am referring to is found in Matthew 14:22-36:

> Immediately Jesus made the disciples get into the boat and go on ahead of him to the other side, while he dismissed the crowd. After he had dismissed them, he went up on a mountainside by himself to pray. Later that night, he was there alone, and the boat was already a considerable distance from land, buffeted by the waves because the wind was against it.

Shortly before dawn Jesus went out to them, walking on the lake. When the disciples saw him walking on the lake, they were terrified. "It's a ghost," they said, and cried out in fear. But Jesus immediately said to them: "Take courage! It is I. Don't be afraid."

"Lord, if it's you," Peter replied, "tell me to come to you on the water."

"Come," he said.

Then Peter got down out of the boat, walked on the water and came toward Jesus. But when he saw the wind, he was afraid and, beginning to sink, cried out, "Lord, save me!"

Immediately Jesus reached out his hand and caught him. "You of little faith," he said, "why did you doubt?"

And when they climbed into the boat, the wind died down. Then those who were in the boat worshiped him, saying, "Truly you are the Son of God."

When they had crossed over, they landed at Gennesaret. And when the men of that place recognized Jesus, they sent word to all the surrounding country. People brought all their sick to him and begged him to let the sick just touch the edge of his cloak, and all who touched it were healed.

All of this happened just after Jesus had fed thousands of people with only a few fish and loaves of bread. It would be difficult to overstate the magnitude of what had occurred. After a full day of ministering to a great multitude of people, Jesus had miraculously multiplied the fish and loaves to feed them! No doubt, neither the disciples nor anyone else had ever witnessed anything even remotely close to this display. Imagine the sense of sheer excitement that must have permeated the atmosphere of that deserted place when people started to realize what was happening! One by one, they began to take part in what was quite literally a supernatural feast. Imagine, as well, the elation that the disciples must have felt as they worked hard to organize and help distribute the *miracle meal* to the awe-struck crowd. They were no doubt reveling in the victory of that day when Jesus instructed them to get into the boat and cross over to the other side.

There is so much meaning that can be mined out of these verses if we are willing to do the work. And there is so much rich application that can help us to sail through not only the storms of our lives but the smooth waters as well. The Greek word used in these verses that instructed the disciples to cross over to the other side is the word *peran*. It comes from a root word *peiro* which means "to pierce through" and "go farther." This picture of piercing through assumes that there is a barrier that must be breached in order to continue moving forward.

IDENTIFY YOUR BARRIERS

What is hindering you? What barriers do you face that keep you from moving forward in your life? Even though the disciples would likely have preferred to have a restful evening celebrating the incredible miracles they had witnessed that day, Jesus challenged them to cross over to the other side. In the same way, I believe that the Lord is constantly challenging each one of us to cross over to the other side—to keep moving forward and not be satisfied with the status quo. This challenge to go farther implies that there is more waiting for you on the other side. No matter what kind of barrier you are up against, you must realize that, by definition, the purpose of a barrier is to obstruct progress. The enemy of your soul will use anything available to obstruct your progress and hinder you from moving forward in your life.

> # Faith is the currency of God's kingdom—and fear is the currency of Satan's kingdom.

One of the most common hindrances we face is the barrier of fear. *Faith is the currency of God's kingdom—and fear is the currency of Satan's kingdom.* Fear, in its various forms, is one of the most common reasons that many people live far below the level of their destiny. Fear of failure has been responsible for paralyzing people from even attempting to follow their God-given dreams. It doesn't make sense when you begin to analyze it. When we allow the possibility of failure to stop us from attempting anything great, failure is no longer just a possibility—it is guaranteed!

"Everything you ever wanted is on the other side of fear."
—George Addair

We all have something in common with the disciples in this story. Our destiny awaits our decision to follow the Lord's instruction to cross over to the other side.

WE CAN'T STAY WHERE WE ARE

There is a principle that we see repeated in Scripture: *We can't stay here.* God spoke to Abram to take his family and leave his homeland to follow the Lord to a place called Canaan. When Abram set out on this journey, he did not know exactly where he was going. He only had a promise that he would receive direction from God.

Centuries later, we see the same principle when God sent Moses to deliver the people of Israel from Egyptian bondage. God's plan was for them to follow Him in obedience to the land that He had promised to give them. But their unbelief and disobedience became the barriers that caused an entire generation to spend their lives wandering in the wilderness when they could have been living a life a blessing and favor in God's promised land!

Crossing over to the other side means that we can't stay where we are. It also means that *we can't stay who we are.* This is another principle that we see repeated in the Scriptures. Over and over, God would take an individual and transform them into a brand-new person with radically different characteristics.

WE CAN'T STAY "WHO" WE ARE

While we can readily see examples of the people of God being led into transitions from one place to another, the greater narrative in the Scriptures is not about transition as much as it is about transformation. It is true, many times, that we can't stay "where" we are, but even more importantly, we can't stay "who" we are. The book of Romans reveals God's stated purposes for our lives: "For those God foreknew he also predestined to be conformed to the image of his Son, that he might be the firstborn among many brothers and sisters" (Romans 8:29).

> The greater narrative in the Scriptures is not about transition as much as it is about transformation.

The word "conformed" in this verse is the Greek word *summorphos*. It means to "be conformed, by sharing the same inner essence or identity." In context, it means that we should display behavior similar to Jesus' because we have the same essential nature. It is important to note that this word does not describe a strictly human attempt at outward conformity to Christ. It indicates an inward change of nature that flows naturally into an outward change of behavior. When Christ comes into our lives, He brings change to the very core of our being. As a result, our outward lifestyle changes as well if we continue to embrace His work in us.

There is another verse in Romans that reveals a deep layer of the Lord's work in us: "Do not conform to the pattern of this world, but be transformed by the renewing of your mind. Then you will be able to test and approve what God's will is—his good, pleasing and perfect will" (Romans 12:2).

The word "transformed" in this verse is the Greek word *metamorphoo*. Sound familiar? It should. This is the root of the English word "metamorphosis." The *Oxford English Dictionary's* definitions of metamorphosis are very revealing:

→ "the process of transformation from an immature form to an adult form in a series of distinct stages [in an insect or amphibian]"

→ "a change of the form or nature of a thing or person into a completely different one, by natural or supernatural means"[2]

I think it is significant that one definition describes the process of transformation from immaturity to maturity. I believe that is why the Holy Spirit chose this specific word to describe the process of

---

2 "Metamorphosis," *Oxford English Dictionary*, OED, 2022, https://www.oed.com/.

transformation that believers go through in their journey from immaturity to maturity in their spiritual lives.

For many people, the first thing that comes to mind when they hear the word metamorphosis is the profound sequence of change that occurs in the life cycle of a caterpillar that causes its transformation into a butterfly. I remember a science project in grade school. We captured some caterpillars and put them in glass jars with twigs and a lot of leaves for them to eat. Then, as the days passed, we observed them moving from the caterpillar stage to the chrysalis stage. We watched and waited with great anticipation for the day when each chrysalis would burst open, and out would come a beautiful, colorful butterfly! It seemed like magic to a group of elementary school kids. We could not fathom how a little worm-like creature could stuff itself by eating constantly and then form a hardened chamber in which it would basically be reduced to a semiliquid state. Then as the structural features of the butterfly began to form, it would emerge with virtually no characteristics of its former self. Metamorphosis is not about minor tweaks or outward adjustments; it is a complete and total transformation from the inside out.

It is interesting to note that everything—every bit of DNA and every molecule of genetic material—needed to produce a creature that could take flight and soar on the winds was *always* present within that chubby little caterpillar.

This should be very encouraging to all of us. Even if you think you'll never be anything but a caterpillar resigned to a life of creeping around stuffing yourself with leaves, the design for the version of you that can take flight is already in the mind of the One who created you. What you need is a metamorphosis. What I need is a metamorphosis. It's what we *all* need. We all need that supernatural transformation from the inside out. Too often, we try to affect a change in our outward behavior, only to find that we are fighting a losing battle because our inward self remains the same. How often have we declared a decision to muster up willpower for a change in our life, only to realize soon afterward that there was no power in our will.

If you think it is encouraging to engage the subject of metamorphosis and talk about the potential for significant life change, I'm inclined to interject the standard late-night infomercial hook at this point: "But wait—there's more!" As we often find, even the most profound revelations derived simply from our English translations of the Bible fail to transmit all of the truth that is contained in the original text. This is one of those times. There is a nuance in the Greek text that escapes our attention in the English translations. Specifically, the word *metamorphoo* is a compound word that literally means "transformed after being with."

The context into which this word is placed in Romans 12:1-2 is instructing us to present ourselves to God as a living sacrifice. In other words, we willingly and eagerly present our lives to Him. This, of necessity, includes a commitment on our part to abide in His presence! And it is in that context, that the Bible says that we are to be "transformed by the renewing of our mind." As we spend time in His presence, our minds are renewed, and our thinking is transformed. When those changes happen inwardly, it clears the way for changes outwardly. Metamorphosis happens because we are literally "transformed after being with Him." His presence in our life changes us from the inside/out. And slowly crawling, leaf-eating caterpillars become beautifully colored, wind-surfing butterflies! The caterpillar was never meant to stay in that stage. The design was always for it to take flight and live an entirely new kind of life. We were never meant to stay the same, either. God's design was always for us to be transformed from the inside/out so that we could live an entirely new kind of life—a life of beauty and the breeze.

We see examples of this kind of transformation all through the Scriptures.

God transformed Abram into Abraham.

In Genesis 11 and 12, we are introduced to a character named Abram. God had spoken to Abram and called him to a very specific destiny. The call on Abram's life was, in essence, to leave his comfortable surroundings of family and friends and step out in faith to journey to a destination and a destiny for which God had created him. Abram demonstrated an amazing depth of faith in God. He routinely chose to step out in faith and follow God's direction when doing so required him to embrace uncertainty and, many times, an extreme level of discomfort. God promised Abram that he would be the father of a nation, and Abram believed God's promise in spite of his advanced age.

In Genesis 17, God made a special covenant with Abram and changed his name to Abraham which means "father of a multitude." At the time of this covenant, Abraham was already ninety-nine years old. His wife, Sarah, was also well past child-bearing years. One of the foundational statements of the entire Old Testament is found in Genesis 15:6 (NKJV): "And [Abraham] believed in the Lord, and He accounted it to him for righteousness." There is much more to the story, but we will leave that narrative for now. The overview of Abraham's life portrays a man who could have remained in a comfortable place in his life but instead chose to step out in faith and follow the Lord. That decision forever altered the course of his life and led him to fulfill an amazing destiny that not only transformed his life but literally changed the world as his descendants became the nation of Israel.

God transformed Jacob into Israel.
One of the most powerful narratives in the Old Testament is the story of the life of Jacob. Jacob was the grandson of Abraham and the son of Isaac. Isaac, of course, was the promised son that was born to Abraham and Sarah in their old age. Isaac's wife Rebekah bore twin sons, Esau and Jacob. From the moment of his birth, Jacob carried a negative label. His very name invokes the idea that he was a deceiver. And as often happens, he lived up to the negative expectations that were placed upon him.

Jacob is the focus of some of the most well-known stories in the Old Testament: stories that detail how he deceived his aged father and stole his brother's birthright and blessing. But God saw much more in Jacob than the mistakes that he made. One night, as he wrestled with the prospect of facing Esau for the first time in years, another struggle ensued. Jacob's life had been a series of struggles. His mother Rebekah's pregnancy was evidently a very difficult one, so much so, that it seemed that her twins were wrestling in her womb.

Jacob later struggled in apparent competition with his brother for his father's approval. Next, he struggled with his uncle, Laban, who taught Jacob what it was like to be on the receiving end of deception. Then, right before his impending encounter with Esau, he faced the struggle of his life as he wrestled with the Lord. It was in that encounter with the Lord that Jacob's life was forever changed. He displayed an admirable courage and a refusal to give up that was commended by his divine opponent. Even after having his hip displaced, he still persevered.

There are several powerful lessons that come to light as we examine this story. Why did the angel of the Lord ask Jacob his name? He most certainly already knew his name. I believe that the reason Jacob was asked his name is that to answer that question, he would be forced to admit who he was. He had to voice the fact that he was Jacob (supplanter, deceiver). The lesson here is simple: in order to access anything that God has for us, we first have to admit the truth about who we are. If I am not willing to admit my need, I cannot access God's supply.

> In order to access anything that God has for us, we first have to admit the truth about who we are.

It was at this point that Jacob's entire life took a major turn! God spoke a word that began one of the most drastic transformations seen in the Scriptures. The Lord told him from that point on, his name would no longer be Jacob. Going forward, he would be known as Israel. God essentially changed his label from that of a deceiver to a name that means "prince with God"! This man, whose life had been filled with chaos and struggle, would become the father of the children of Israel! That's an amazing metamorphosis! God gave Jacob a new name, a new walk (thanks to his hip injury), and a new opportunity to live out a divine destiny beyond his wildest dreams.

God transformed Saul into Paul.

There are many other examples in the Bible of radical transformation in the lives of people who had a powerful encounter with God. But for our purposes, we will address just one more. This is the transformation that happened in the life of Saul of Tarsus. Tarsus was a Greek city that was a prosperous center of education and philosophy. Saul was raised in two worlds; Greek culture and Jewish culture were both part of his upbringing. Saul was not only a Jew but was raised in the strict disciplines of the Pharisees. He was very zealous for Judaism and the Law.

When the new sect of Christ-followers sprang up, he viewed it as heresy and was violently opposed to the Christian message. By his own admission, he eagerly rounded up followers of Jesus and had them thrown into prison. Then, one day while he was on his way to Damascus, a blinding light startled Saul, and he fell to the ground. Acts 26:14 (NLT) tells us he heard God's voice say, "Saul, Saul, why are you persecuting me?" He quickly humbled himself and asked for God's direction. God allowed Saul, who had been spiritually blind to be physically blind for a short time to punctuate his need for change.

God confirmed with Saul and others that it was his destiny to bring the gospel message to the gentiles as well as the Jews. In response to this radical transformation from persecutor to preacher: Saul's name was changed to Paul. Once again, a powerful encounter with God brought about an amazing transformation in the life of a person who was far away from the path of his divine destiny. We have only examined a few examples from Scripture, but there are countless other examples of this kind of metamorphosis in people's lives down through the centuries. And they are still happening today!

METAMORPHOSIS STILL HAPPENS

It is very likely that you have witnessed this type of metamorphosis in someone else. God is still transforming people's lives. There was a teenage boy in my freshman class in high school who was a clear example of metamorphosis. He came from a good home, made good grades, and was active in extra-curricular activities. But like many others, he found himself caught up in an intense struggle with peer pressure. His desire to be accepted led him down a path of alcohol and drug use. His experience was typical in many ways, in that he ended up doing things he didn't necessarily want to do, just to be popular and accepted.

Near the end of his freshman year, a student photographer was taking pictures for the yearbook and snapped a photo of him coming in the back door of the school with glazed, bloodshot eyes and a "stoned surfer" look on his face. He had been with a group of students that used to meet out behind the school to get high before class. He had no idea that evidence of his condition would be caught on film. He also had no idea that this unflattering photo would end up in the yearbook.

Then, everything changed! Just a month after summer break began, a girl that he had liked for years invited him to a church youth rally at a town nearby. Because he liked this girl, he agreed to go. His only motivation at that point was to spend time with her. He was totally unaware that he would have a divine encounter with God that night— one that would change the trajectory of his entire life!

During the service, he felt a strong sense of God's presence and a deep conviction that he needed to change his ways and get serious about a real relationship with God. He responded to the altar call that night and gave his life to Christ! The change was obvious and immediate. The small group of teens from the church started a Bible quiz team that summer, and he joined. The daily discipline of studying and memorizing large portions of the gospel of John was the exact prescription that this young man needed to propel him into fast-growth mode in his spiritual life.

His radical transformation became evident to students and teachers once classes had resumed in the fall. This young man was so completely different that everyone's perception of him changed. The evidence of metamorphosis in his life was so compelling that he went from being viewed as one of "those" kids out behind the school to being elected president of his junior class!

And the transformation continued to affect every aspect of his life: from his attitude to his demeanor and even his dreams and goals. He shifted his plans from a career in autobody paint and repair to following a call to ministry. You may be wondering how I know so much about that young man and why I have relayed this entire narrative without ever once using his name. By now, you have likely guessed that I'm aware of so much detail about his life because that young man was me.

When I talk about metamorphosis, I am not just repeating what I have heard others say. I was blessed to have experienced first-hand this amazing, life-altering change. My name was not "literally" changed like the examples we cited earlier from the Bible, but my name *was* changed in the very real sense that my character and reputation were transformed.

God's stated purpose for our lives is transformation. He delights in seeing us progress from one level to the next until we reach the peak of our potential to become all that He designed us to be. At the beginning of this chapter, you were prompted to identify the barriers in your life. Barriers exist to paralyze our progress and derail our destiny in God's kingdom. We are called to cross over, and we must not allow the barriers to stop us. What is in your heart that God has called you to become? There is an ultimate version of you that God wants to bring out. And He is waiting for you to answer the call, to cross over to the other side.

> God's stated purpose for our lives is transformation.

REFLECTION & APPLICATION

1) What is the next step in your spiritual journey that God is leading you to take?

2) What barriers are hindering your progress, and how is God leading you to address those issues?

3) What image has God imprinted in your mind of the version of you that can take flight and soar above the landscape of your past?

4) Regularly spending time in the presence of God can lead to a metamorphosis in your life that brings God's vision for you into full reality. If you alter your schedule to include an altar of time in God's presence, He will alter your life to soar above your past! Why not create your new daily schedule now?

SAMPLE PRAYER

Lord, I thank You for reminding me that You have not created me to sit and stagnate. You have called me to follow You in a daily journey of crossing over to the other side and piercing through the barriers that hinder my destiny. Please help me to invest time every day in Your presence so that you can transform me into the ultimate version that You have created me to become. Help me to identify the barriers that I need to break through in order to keep growing in my relationship with You. I pray these things in the mighty name of Jesus! Amen.

FAITH DECLARATION

Lord, I declare by faith that I will answer Your call on my life to move forward and grow in You. I will invest significant amounts of time in prayer, worship, and the study of Your Word, so that my mind can be renewed and my life can be transformed into the image of Christ. I declare that every hindrance that stands in my way will fall before me as Goliath fell before David. May my life be a compelling example of metamorphosis that will bring me into my highest destiny and give all the glory to You. I declare these things by faith in the name of Jesus!

CHAPTER 3

SENT INTO THE STORM

Not long after Jesus had instructed His disciples to cross over to the other side of the lake, a severe storm engulfed them, and they found themselves fighting for their lives against unexpected wind and waves. No one likes adversity. In fact, a universal trait that human beings share is the tendency to avoid difficulty and resistance. We love our comfort zones, and we do everything in our power to stay there.

But everyone goes through storms in life. Some of those storms are of our own brewing while others have no connection at all to choices that we have made. I believe that Jesus sent the disciples across the lake, knowing that a storm was coming. I've often wondered if someone in the boat raised the question, "Why in the world did Jesus send us into this mess?" Have you ever asked that question? I know I have. Not all storms in life are the result of disobedience. Sometimes, following God's will can take us right into the pathway of adversity.

> Not all storms in life are the result of
> disobedience. Sometimes, following God's will
> can take us right into the pathway of adversity.

A LINE OF STORMS

As I mentioned earlier, Colton's story showcases just a fraction of the troubles our family has faced. Less than a year after Colton's second open-heart surgery, my wife, Nancy, almost died from an autoimmune disease. We had noticed mysterious bruises appearing all over her body, so we called her doctor and set an appointment for the following morning. On the way into the appointment, she lost consciousness and had to be taken into the office in a wheelchair. A few minutes later, they transported her across the street to the hospital emergency room.

As I nervously sat in the waiting room, her doctor came out and told me that Nancy was about to be taken into emergency surgery. They had discovered that her blood platelet count was less than 2000. A normal count would have been between 150,000 and 450,000. She was literally bleeding to death internally, and we'd had no clue. Her doctor told me that if we had been twenty minutes later arriving at his office she would have died. I could not believe what I was hearing. Nancy and I had been sweethearts since the second grade, and I could not even imagine life without her!

Thankfully, she survived the procedure, and they were able to get her blood loss under control. But she was still extremely sick, and it was months before the doctors were confident that she would survive. She was bedridden for about six months, and it took several years for her to recover normal life. As she continued to progress, we started the conversation about expanding our family. However, because of her illness, another pregnancy was not an option.

As we prayed about it, we felt the Lord leading us to adopt a baby girl from China. We began the process in the spring of 1999, and almost immediately, we began to encounter setbacks. Paperwork got lost and had to be resubmitted. Then, other documents expired as a result of the delays. Frustrated by the problems, we would pray about them, and each time the Lord would answer: *It's not the right time. She is not the right baby. Just keep the process moving.* So, we did as the Lord instructed.

Nine months after Colton's third open-heart surgery when he was eight years old, the day finally came in March of 2001 when we, along with seven other couples from our adoption agency, boarded a plane bound for China to adopt orphans and bring them home to their forever families. Our celebration was especially exciting because Nancy's sister and her husband were in our group and had also adopted a child from China. We spent two weeks completing all the paperwork, official interviews, and medical exams for the babies. We bonded immediately with our little Chinese princess, Anna Grace. From the moment we first held her, we knew that God had led us to this child and that she had always been destined to be our daughter. She was not even born when we began our paperwork, but all the delays we encountered enabled us to be matched as Anna Grace's adoptive parents.

After the long flight back home, we walked up the Jetway from our plane into the Memphis airport, and the celebration began! We were greeted by our families and at least fifty people from our church, cheering and waving welcome home signs and balloons. That was back in the days before 9/11 when you could actually go to the gate to greet returning passengers. We breathed a great sigh of relief and satisfaction that the long process of adopting our baby girl was finished. But the celebration soon turned to concern because, almost immediately after we landed, Anna Grace got sick.

EVERY PARENT'S WORST NIGHTMARE

We noticed that she seemed to be developing what was commonly known as a lazy eye in that it didn't track with her other eye. Then she started having problems keeping food down and eventually lost the ability to sit up on her own. We took her to the doctor numerous times in the first three weeks after our return from China. Her pediatrician scheduled a CT scan to investigate her issues. And less than a month after we got home with Anna Grace, Nancy and I sat in a room with a doctor whose first words were, "This is every parent's worst nightmare. And I am so sorry to have to inform you that Anna Grace has a large brain tumor."

We absolutely knew that God had orchestrated our path to adopt Anna Grace. His fingerprints were all over the circumstances that connected us with her, and that knowledge was simultaneously encouraging and frustrating. It was encouraging because it was obvious that God was engaged in a plan, but it was also frustrating to see unmistakable evidence of God's involvement in this whole event. If God arranged every detail to guarantee that we adopted Anna Grace, why didn't He just miraculously heal her? After everything we had already been through with our family's health—we could not believe that we had been sent into another storm! There are tough questions that we wrestle with when the storms of life surround us. But we can't afford to get stuck in our unanswered questions.

No doubt, you have experienced seasons of adversity in your life that you did not understand. It is easy for us to connect the dots when adversity results from dumb decisions or bad choices that we have made. But it is always a challenge for us to try to understand why God allows a storm to engulf our lives when we are walking in obedience to His will. As we look into the Scriptures, it becomes apparent that it is actually normal to face resistance after a decision to obey God.

> ## As we look into the Scriptures, it becomes apparent that it is actually normal to face resistance after a decision to obey God.

OBEDIENCE FOLLOWED BY ADVERSITY

When Moses obeyed God's command to go back to Egypt to lead God's people out of bondage, he faced obstacle after obstacle in the process. Pharaoh repeatedly refused to let the people go—until God punctuated the demand with an ever-escalating series of plagues that ultimately convinced Pharaoh to comply. Then, upon Israel's departure, Pharaoh changed his mind and sent the armies of Egypt in pursuit of the Hebrews, who suddenly found themselves trapped between the armies of Pharaoh and the Red Sea.

Don't you think at that moment that Moses was confused? *Why in the world would God send us into this mess?* The Red Sea seemed like an uncrossable barrier before them as certain death pursued them from behind. Then God did what God does! He made a way where there was no way. He opened the Red Sea in front of them and delayed their enemies until Israel had safely crossed over to the other side. Moses' obedience to God's plan ultimately brought the people of Israel to the border of the Promised Land, but the process could in no way be described as smooth sailing. When we choose to step out in faith and obey God's instructions, a time of testing typically follows.

We find another example of this principle in the story of Shadrach, Meshach and Abednego in Daniel 3. They had served King Nebuchadnezzar faithfully in administrating the affairs of the province, but when the king challenged their allegiance to God and demanded that they worship his gods and his golden image, they chose to do the right thing. They refused to worship anyone except the God of Israel. This decision was a courageous act of obedience to God, but it also landed them in the fiery furnace! They expressed an amazing attitude of faith when they told the king that God was able to deliver them from the furnace—but even if He did not choose to rescue them, they still would not bow down to false gods.

As they were thrown into the middle of the fire, God did what God does. He showed up in the furnace and protected them from any harm! The end of this story reveals some interesting details.

Then King Nebuchadnezzar leaped to his feet in amazement and asked his advisers, "Weren't there three men that we tied up and threw into the fire?"

They replied, "Certainly, Your Majesty."

He said, "Look! I see four men walking around in the fire, unbound and unharmed, and the
fourth looks like a son of the gods."

Nebuchadnezzar then approached the opening of the blazing furnace and shouted, "Shadrach, Meshach and Abednego, servants of the Most High God, come out! Come here!"

So Shadrach, Meshach and Abednego came out of the
fire, and the satraps, prefects, governors and royal advisers
crowded around them. They saw that the fire had not harmed
their bodies, nor was a hair of their heads singed, their robes
were not scorched, and there was no smell of fire on them.
—Daniel 3:24-27

What started out as three men bound and thrown into the furnace ended up as four men loose and walking around among the flames! The fourth man in the fire was none other than the Lord Himself. So, how did they get loose? Did the Lord remove their bonds within the furnace, or did He allow the fire to burn away the things that bound them while protecting them from any personal harm? I can't say for certain, but I have seen in my own life and in the lives of others that if we choose to keep our eyes on the Lord instead of the flames—he can use the flames of adversity to burn away the things in our lives that bind us while protecting us from destruction. If you find yourself in the furnace of adversity, keep your focus on the Lord (who is with you in the fire), and ask Him to burn away the things that have bound you.

Have you ever wondered why the men were just walking around inside the furnace once they were free from their restraints? Did you notice that they didn't even attempt to leave the furnace until the king called them out? Why would they choose to stay in the fire when they were free to leave? Could it be that the presence of God was so amazing as they walked with Him among the flames that they were in no hurry to leave? I can tell you from personal experience that there have been times when we were in the middle of a fiery trial that threatened to destroy our family, but the presence of God that surrounded us was so tangible that we experienced what the Bible describes as a peace that passes all understanding. In some of the darkest days of our lives, we have had people ask us how we could possibly still have the joy of the Lord. The reason was because even though we were in the furnace of adversity, we were not alone. The Lord made His presence and peace so real that we experienced the reality of Psalm 16:11 (NKJV), "In [His] presence is fullness of joy."

Then, when the men's fiery test was over, it was time for their testimony. As they strolled out of the flames, everyone was amazed. The fire had not harmed them at all. Their bodies sustained no burns, their hair was not singed, their robes were not scorched, and they didn't even smell like smoke! That may be the biggest miracle in this story. I can't even grill burgers without smelling like I've been in a fiery furnace! From the Scriptures, it is evident that obedience is often followed by a time of testing. And thankfully, the time of testing is followed by a moment of victory!

In Acts 16, the story of Paul and Silas in prison is a prime example of God's presence in our trials. Paul and Silas encountered a young slave girl possessed by an evil spirit. Her owners made a lot of money from her fortune-telling skills, and when Paul cast the demon out of the girl, her owners stirred up the crowds, and the authorities put Paul and Silas in prison. Obedience to God's call led them directly into a time of testing.

When reading all these examples in the Bible, I've often imagined the magnitude of the pity party that I would have pitched if I had been Moses, the three Hebrews in the furnace, or Paul and Silas in jail for ministering the gospel powerfully. Full disclosure: Nancy and I have actually engaged in a few pity parties and depression sessions along the pathway that we have walked. But we don't find Paul and Silas in complaint mode. After having been beaten severely and chained up in the jail, we find them worshiping God.

About midnight Paul and Silas were praying and singing hymns to God, and the other prisoners were listening to them. Suddenly there was such a violent earthquake that the foundations of the prison were shaken. At once all the prison doors flew open, and everyone's chains came loose. The jailer woke up, and when he saw the prison doors open, he drew his sword and was about to kill himself because he thought the prisoners had escaped. But Paul shouted, "Don't harm yourself! We are all here!"

The jailer called for lights, rushed in and fell trembling before Paul and Silas. He then brought them out and asked, "Sirs, what must I do to be saved?" —Acts 16:25-30

Acts 16:25 states: "At midnight, Paul and Silas were praying and singing hymns to God and the other prisoners were listening to them." In many genres of literature, midnight has long been a metaphor for darkness and despair. They were in the prison at midnight, but instead of complaining, they chose to worship. And their worship captured the attention of all the other prisoners. You might imagine that worship in the prison was not a common occurrence. Shouting, arguing, fighting, cursing . . . sure—but not worshiping. It was the difference in Paul and Silas's attitude that got the attention of others. If you can worship God in the middle of your midnight—you will impact the lives of everyone around you!

> If you can worship God in the middle of your midnight—you will impact the lives of everyone around you!

The Bible states that as they worshiped God, an earthquake shook the foundations of the prison and "all the doors flew open and everyone's chains fell off" (Acts 16:26). Did you get that? Everyone's chains fell off! Paul and Silas were not the only ones affected by their choice to offer the sacrifice of praise. Their commitment to worshiping God in spite of their circumstances made a huge impact on all the other prisoners. No doubt, the timing of the earthquake was miraculous, but another miracle would follow.

When the jailer came in and saw all the doors open, he immediately drew his sword and was about to kill himself. He assumed that everyone had escaped, and if that were true, he would have faced a torturous punishment. But Paul shouted, "Do not harm yourself. We are all here." That was a miracle. Open the prison doors and nobody leaves? Why? I wonder if this was a situation similar to what we see in the story of the fiery furnace. Could it be that no one wanted to leave the powerful presence of God that was inhabiting the praises of Paul and Silas? They possessed a genuine spirit of joy in the middle of circumstances that no one would choose.

As I mentioned earlier, I know what this is like. Nancy and I have experienced it many times in the middle of the trials and troubles that we have endured. During some of the darkest days of our lives, we have experienced a keen awareness of the comforting presence of the Holy Spirit in ways that are difficult to explain. Many times in our lives, we have felt as though we were living in a *cocoon* of God's grace. And that grace enabled us to make it through those seasons. Often, people would ask us how we were surviving—the truth was we were actually thriving.

One powerful lesson in all these examples is this: God is with you in your troubles! Hebrews 13:5 says that God has said He would not leave us nor forsake us, and He is true to His Word. The title of this chapter is "Sent into the Storm" because in every example we highlighted, it was obedience to God's instructions that led to the challenges. We need to remember that the Lord never guaranteed us a life of smooth sailing because God's divine destiny for us often requires a pathway through the storm as evidenced by 1 Peter 4:12: "Dear friends, do not be surprised at the fiery ordeal that has come on you to test you, as though something strange were happening to you."

> We need to remember that the Lord never guaranteed us a life of smooth sailing because God's divine destiny for us often requires a pathway through the storm.

If we perceive our troubles and challenges as a normal part of life in this fallen world, we are more likely to trust the Lord to carry us through the storms instead of blaming Him for them. In John, Jesus was preparing His disciples for the turmoil they were about to face during His crucifixion and death. As He was sharing some of the events that were on the horizon, He clarified a truth that we must always remember: "I have told you these things, so that in me you may have peace. In this world you will have trouble. But take heart! I have overcome the world" (John 16:33).

Take note of the phrase "in me you may have peace." Jesus spent a considerable amount of time in John 15 teaching His disciples that they must learn to abide in him. When we abide in Christ, we can be at peace even in the middle of a crisis. When we choose to view our trials as a normal part of life on earth, we are freeing ourselves from the devil's trap of interpreting everything through the lens of *this should not be happening to me.* When we fall into the trap of that perception, we can begin to harbor offense in our hearts towards the Lord, and that can be very dangerous to our spiritual health. Keeping a proper perspective on the events of our lives empowers us to keep moving forward through every storm.

Now might be a good time for us to revisit my story about the butterfly metamorphosis science project in the previous chapter. I saved one detail of that story to interject at an appropriate place. When it came time for the butterfly to emerge from the chrysalis, there was something that became a concern to us. It seemed to us that the butterfly was struggling to try to break open the chrysalis. We were excited at the prospect of seeing this little miracle emerge right before our eyes. In our anticipation, we grew more impatient as the minutes passed of watching the chrysalis shake from side to side as the butterfly moved around inside trying to break open its tiny prison.

At this point, we began to ask our teacher if there was anything we could do to help our little struggling friend escape. We were told that we should be patient and let the process happen naturally the way it was intended. It seemed like it would be the *kind* thing to do if we could somehow cut a little slit in the chrysalis to make it easier for the butterfly to extract itself. But what *seems* like the kind thing to do may not always be for the best.

The truth is that the process of the butterfly exiting the chrysalis has actually been designed to include struggle. The struggle against the resistance of the encasement actually prepares the butterfly for flight. The strain of the struggle helps pump fluid from the abdomen of the newly formed butterfly into the wings in order to inflate them. The struggle also strengthens the wings to help prepare them for use. Without the struggle, the butterfly might not even be able to fly. And without the power of flight, it likely would not survive for very long against its natural predators. So, the next time you get aggravated because you feel like the Lord has sent you directly into a storm, remember, it may very well be the struggle of today that provides the strength you will need for tomorrow.

It is the process of the fight that empowers you for flight!

> It is the process of the fight that empowers you for flight!

REFLECTION & APPLICATION

1) Can you describe a time in your life when you felt like you had been sent into a storm?

2) What was your greatest struggle during the season you just described?

3) Can you describe a time in your life when you have experienced a God-given peace that did not make sense when compared with your circumstances?

SAMPLE PRAYER

Lord, I thank You for Your promise to never leave me nor forsake me. I know that Your presence is always with me, even in times when I don't understand my circumstances. You taught us in Your Word that we would have trouble in this world, and You never promised us a life of smooth sailing. But You also taught us to take courage because You have overcome the world. Lord, I choose to abide in You—to live in Your presence, today and every day. In those times when I don't understand my circumstances, I choose to trust in You rather than get bogged down in my unanswered questions. In Jesus' name, I pray. Amen.

FAITH DECLARATION

Lord, I declare by faith that no matter what trials and tribulations come my way, You will never leave me nor forsake me. Your presence will always be with me—in good times and bad times. I choose to take courage in You, knowing that You can overcome every attack that I will ever experience. I choose to abide in Your presence, and even when I don't understand why I have been sent into a storm, I will keep my trust in You as my Savior. I declare these things by faith in the name of Jesus!

CHAPTER 4

ROUGH SEAS: THE STRENGTH OF THE STORM

*"After he had dismissed them, he went up on a mountainside
by himself to pray. Later that night, he was there alone,
and the boat was already a considerable distance from land,
buffeted by the waves because the wind was against it."*
—Matthew 14:23-24

A s we have already seen, in the time it took Jesus to climb the mountain to pray, the disciples were already a great distance from land. If you have ever been in a boat on a large body of water, you know that the closer you are to the land, the better your sense of security. They were a long way from land—and a long way from comfort and safety. The path that Jesus sent them on took them far from their comfort zones. Sound familiar? I'm sure it does.

We *love* our comfort zones. An honest examination of our prayer lives would likely reveal a lot of prayers asking God to remove obstacles, take away trials, fix our problems, and eliminate all forms of resistance in our lives. I know I have prayed my fair share of *comfort zone prayers.* The problem comes when we want God to *change* our circumstances, but God wants to *use* our circumstances to change us. Raise your hand if you've ever daydreamed about having a totally problem-free life. It's really hard to type with one hand in the air, isn't it!

On the surface, *problem-free* sounds awesome—until you think it through. When I was about twelve years old, my dad fell off a truck and broke his arm. He was in a cast for about six weeks. I still remember the day he came home from the doctor's office after having the cast removed. My dad was always a big man with decent-sized biceps. But when he walked into the house, and I saw his arm without the cast, I laughed out loud. It literally looked like the doctor had transplanted some skinny guy's arm onto Dad's shoulder. It seemed about half as big as his other arm. For six weeks, the muscles in that arm had been immobilized and had experienced no resistance. That lack of resistance caused the muscles to atrophy. When we don't use our spiritual muscles to face trials, we don't get to experience the strength God wants us to build into our lives. Whether we like it or not, facing resistance will always be important for us.

In their journey across the lake, the disciples had reached what could be called the point of no return. They were a long way from either shore when the storm developed suddenly. That region is very susceptible to storms that form quickly and sweep down the mountains toward the Sea of Galilee. The Bible says the winds were *against* them, and the boat was being *buffeted* by the waves. They were in a situation that was out of their control. The winds were blowing forcefully against them. In other words, they were experiencing direct opposition to Jesus' instructions to cross over to the other side. Have you ever felt like the winds of life were blowing against you? I'll bet you have.

PREDICTABLE RESISTANCE

Navigating our storms has taught us to think of opposition in life as *predictable resistance*. It's not unusual—it's normal. One of the reasons that we tend to interpret resistance negatively is because we value comfort above almost everything else. But God views our lives from a much higher perspective, and He sees the potential benefit for us in facing opposition.

Building character is not unlike building muscle. The fastest process to build physical strength includes consistently challenging our muscles to the point of failure and then maintaining proper nutrition while we allow them to rest and recover. When we experience the predictable resistance that life often brings, many times, we feel like we are being pushed to the point of failure. Abiding in Christ is vital to our spiritual nutrition and enables us to get stronger and become more spiritually mature in our character.

> Decisions that we make in obedience to the Lord will not go unchallenged.

It is not just important to overcome resistance. We need to overcome resistance the right way. Proper form in the gym helps to build strength faster and avoid injury. To successfully navigate the storms of life also requires that we keep proper form in our perspective.

Decisions that we make in obedience to the Lord will not go unchallenged. This is hard to understand until we realize that God's agenda for His people is not just about believing—it is about becoming. It is not just about arriving at our destination; it is about flourishing in our destiny.

> God's agenda is not only about believing, it is about becoming. It's not just about a destination—it's about a destiny!

The Bible says in Matthew 14:24 that the waves were crashing violently or beating against the boat. Their boat was being tossed around by the waves. Have you ever felt like life was beating on you and tossing you around—far beyond your ability to control? The Greek word translated here as "buffeted" actually means "to torture." I can assure you that there have been many times that I felt like I was being tortured by the trials and tribulations that were beating against us and threatening to capsize our family.

EVERY PARENT'S WORST NIGHTMARE—AGAIN

Just a few hours after Anna Grace's brain tumor was discovered, we cried and prayed over her as they wheeled her away into a 12-hour emergency surgery. For the first several hours, it seemed unlikely that they were going to be able to remove the entire tumor. Then, in their words, "All of a sudden everything changed." The lead surgeon said it was almost as if the tumor *gave up* its hold on Anna's brain. It was obvious that what happened during Anna's surgery was extremely unusual.

We knew that God had supernaturally intervened in Anna's surgery to loosen the tumor. Our minds went back to a report we'd heard from the previous night. This was before the days of social media, but when we received the news about Anna's brain tumor, word quickly spread through the church. About 150 people spontaneously gathered at the church to pray. In a way, what happened in Anna's surgery mirrored what had happened in that prayer meeting the night before. For most of the prayer time, the atmosphere was negatively charged with devastation and discouragement, but then, "All of a sudden everything changed." And a spirit of victory and rejoicing exploded in the auditorium. Everyone knew at that point that God was going to intervene, and Anna Grace would be healed!

It is vital during the storms of life that you have people who love and care about you to stand with you and support you in prayer. Overcoming resistance is far more difficult and dangerous when we attempt it alone, so make sure that you are maintaining close, healthy relationships with God and His people. Our friends stood with us as we anticipated the results of the procedure. We stood beside her crib in the ICU and prayed while we waited for her to wake up. We begged the Lord to give us a sign that Anna was okay—that our baby girl was still *in there.*

Then it happened! We asked for a sign and could not have received a better one. Anna Grace had no interest in pacifiers, but she had a very unique way of sucking her fingers. It was quite complicated and may be difficult to explain without a diagram. She would suck the middle two fingers of her left hand. After the fingers were in place, she would then position her right hand facing away from her, between her chin and her left hand and then interlock her fingers together. Wait . . . there's more. She would then rotate the whole apparatus to her left so that she could rub the tip of her nose with her left pinky finger.

We had never seen anything like it before, but that was her method, and she never deviated from it. As we stood there and prayed, we could tell that she was waking up. She was still groggy, but she started trying to get those two fingers into her mouth. At first, she kept poking herself in the forehead, but after a couple of attempts—she nailed it! Those fingers went in, and she successfully performed the rest of the sequence, complete with the nose-rubbing pinky. We melted into a pool of tears mixed with gratitude to see the sign that our baby girl was still her wonderful self after undergoing an incredibly dangerous and complex procedure.

With the surgery complete, the next focus was the pathology report. This was huge because if the tumor were benign, Anna Grace would be spared the ordeal of further treatment, and we could attempt a return to normal life. We waited a few days, and then came the news that we prayed we would never hear. Less than a month after bringing our baby girl home from China, she was diagnosed with brain cancer. We literally could not comprehend why God was allowing us to be faced with yet another devastating storm.

Anna Grace was immediately transferred to St. Jude Children's Research Hospital. The assessments began, and the next few days were filled with more frightening consultations. We were told that Anna Grace would have to endure about a year of chemotherapy and radiation treatments. We were given long lists of potentially devastating side effects that were possible not only from the tumor but also because of the treatment itself. At one point, a doctor said to us, "Killing the cancer is not the problem. Killing the cancer without damaging her brain is the problem."

There were no guarantees that Anna Grace would ever be able to speak, understand language, walk, feed herself, or perform basic functions of any sort. She had less than a 15 percent chance of survival and virtually no chance of a normal life. To say that we struggled with unanswered questions would be a huge understatement. As weary as we were from all the crises we had been through prior to this event, we realized that the experience we gained through all the other storms had taught us valuable lessons that would help us to deal with this challenge.

We navigated our first few days at St. Jude, and Anna Grace began her treatment. Surgeons installed a port in Anna's chest through which she would receive most of her chemo. They also used it to draw her blood for analysis, so they would not have to stick her with needles every day. There were actually two small white tubes sticking out of her chest, and we were responsible for making sure that those lines were flushed and sterilized every day. It was terrifying to be responsible for the care of her lines because they were inserted directly into her main arteries, and if they got infected, it could kill her. We were told that by the end of Anna's treatment, we would deserve "honorary" nursing degrees because of all we would have to learn to care for Anna properly.

ONE DAY AT A TIME

During the majority of Anna's treatment, we had appointments at St. Jude 3 to 4 days a week. We were very grateful to live so close to the best hospital in the world for childhood cancer. But we were also overwhelmed at the responsibility of leading a growing church that was preparing for a major expansion while walking through this process with Anna Grace. It was so daunting that we had to discipline ourselves not to think about it. Our focus every day was *that* day. When we made it through that day, then we would focus on the next one.

> Our focus every day was that day. When we made it through that day, then we would focus on the next one.

The complex logistics of our schedule over the summer made us question how we could function when Colton started back to school in August. After praying and seeking wise counsel, we decided to homeschool him for his third-grade year. That gave us the flexibility to handle Anna's appointments and spend several hours each day working with Colton. At first, we were concerned about how all of this would affect him. He had already been through so much himself, having just turned nine years old and already having endured three open-heart surgeries. Any concerns we had about Colton having to spend every day at St. Jude vanished quickly. Suffering can tend to create a greater sense of compassion for others, and Colton was a wonderfully compassionate boy. Now, he was being exposed to children with no hair, missing limbs, missing eyes, and all sorts of other issues. But rather than seeing them as weird or *less than*, he viewed them with compassion.

When Anna Grace began her treatment, the doctors expected her to require a feeding tube because the chemotherapy drugs would likely cause her to have chronic nausea. This became another sign that God was going to help Anna Grace. There had never been a baby on her protocol that was able to endure the treatment without a feeding tube—until Anna! Her doctors were astounded at her ability to take the chemo without all the negative side effects. One day, a doctor leaned over, smiled at her and said, "What is your secret?" We informed him that being pastors from the South, we had a two-pronged strategy—prayer plus biscuits and gravy. Anna Grace loved them so much that she actually gained twelve pounds during her treatment! That was unheard of.

We continued our "one day at a time" approach to life as her treatment progressed. After her first twenty weeks of chemo, she entered a six-week period of radiation treatments five days a week. Because we were still doing our best to lead the church through this season, I carried my briefcase to the hospital every day to try to get some work done during the hours I spent in waiting rooms. In the third week of Anna's radiation treatments, I was working in my day planner when suddenly, I was struck with a realization. We were halfway through Anna's treatment! Six months earlier, we could not even comprehend how we would get through this process. But we had been so focused on taking things one day at a time that we lost track of exactly where we were in the process. That realization was incredibly encouraging, and I felt like a weight had been lifted off my shoulders.

Then the Lord began to speak to me about the *power of process*. How are you going to make it through your storm? One day at a time. If you focus on the whole journey, you will feel discouraged and overwhelmed. But you can't do anything about next year, next month, or even next week because you are not there yet. The only day you can influence is today. Pray for God's wisdom and direction. What is the Lord asking of you today? What is His direction for you right now— not tomorrow or next week! Once you set your course and choose your direction, the power of process takes over. If you keep taking one step at a time, you will keep progressing. A single step may seem like nothing, but fifteen minutes of single steps can take you a mile down the road. Stay on course, and you will arrive at your destination.

For over thirty years, I have kept a devotional journal of what is going on in my life and the things God is teaching me. In the process of writing this book, I was researching my journals from 2001 and 2002, and I ran across some cherished entries. Following is a quotation from my journal from the same week as the revelation about the *power of process*. "Wednesday, November 14, 2001: Anna continues to "sail" through her treatment! God has surrounded her with a divine protection from all negative side-effects and impairments from the cancer and from the treatment itself. Thank you, Lord, for helping Anna to grow and develop normally. She is a testimony to your awesome power and grace. Lord, I pray for a great report from Colton's annual cardiology check-up on Thursday. Thank you for healing him and for totally healing Nancy from ITP." The main focus of this chapter has been how we can build strength by overcoming adversity in our lives.

THE UNIVERSITY OF ADVERSITY

Illustration: Please join me in this mental exercise as I believe that it will illustrate the truth of this chapter far better than I could ever do without your involvement.

Think of a person you greatly admire—someone who is such an inspiration to you that your desire is to be like them. You should make your selection based solely on the person's character—who they are—and not for any other reason such as things they possess, fame, or fortune. Feel free to write their name here:_____ _____.

Obviously, I don't have any idea whose name you wrote in that blank. But I do believe that I can provide an accurate description of them. They have suffered a great deal and have persevered through major storms in life. They have come through their tough times stronger and more resilient. And they have maintained a positive outlook despite all their troubles. Why would I venture such a guess about the person you selected?

First, the kind of character that inspires others typically requires a lot of *resistance* to create. Second, I have conducted this illustration in large gatherings and small group settings many times. So far, I have not had anyone tell me that the person they most admire has had an easy life.

Those who are an inspiration to us did not become admirable people by living an easy, stress-free, comfortable, unchallenged existence. They grew into people we admire by conquering obstacles in a healthy way. Overcoming resistance builds strength. Isn't it interesting that the circumstances we prefer are absent of resistance, but the character we hope to develop requires it?

> The circumstances we prefer are absent of resistance, but the character we hope to develop requires it.

Consider with me for a moment the difference in value and desirability between a diamond and a pencil lead. Graphite and diamond are essentially two forms of the same chemical element—carbon. But their physical properties could not be more different. In graphite, the carbon atoms are arranged in sheets that can easily glide against each other. This is the reason that graphite is used in pencils. Graphite molecules slip easily off the pencil onto the paper and leave a black mark.

But in a diamond, the carbon atoms are strongly bonded in all directions. This property is what makes diamonds so extremely hard. When most people think of a diamond, they visualize expensive jewelry, but in the modern age, diamonds have become extremely useful in industrial applications like cutting tools and electronic devices. You have probably already made the connection between the subject of this chapter and the above paragraphs about the various forms of graphite. Transforming graphite into a diamond requires intense heat and pressure over a long period of time. When we choose to trust the Lord in times of intense heat and pressure, both our inner strength and the value of our character are multiplied!

As we rejoin the disciples in their storm on the sea of Galilee, we find that it was the fourth watch of the night when Jesus approached them. It was between 3 a.m. and 6 a.m.—sometime before dawn. This means that the disciples had been struggling to survive this storm all night long. It would be frightening enough to be in a fight for your life out in the raging waters of a stormy sea; it would be even worse to face that storm for several hours in total darkness.

There have been many times when the storm I was facing caused me to feel like I was being engulfed in darkness. But in each case, eventually, the dawn came piercing through and illuminated the situation so that I could see the pathway that God was leading me to walk. No doubt, the disciples were physically exhausted from the long struggle and emotionally confused as to why Jesus would send them into this situation while He stayed behind. The Bible describes other times when the disciples were in a boat on a stormy sea, and Jesus got up and miraculously calmed the storm, but this time, He wasn't in the boat. Why would He purposely let them face this storm while He was not in the boat? We will see the reason for that in a later chapter.

Heat, pressure, and time—sometimes, the heat feels too hot, the pressure seems too great, and the time appears too long. But I have come to believe that in God's agenda, *the higher the heat, the greater the pressure, and the longer the time—the more valuable the treasure.* After our family made it through Anna Grace's battle with cancer, we breathed a sigh of relief, but the season of storms was not over. Three years after Anna Grace finished her treatment, Colton had to endure his fourth open-heart surgery.

> The higher the heat, the greater the pressure, and the longer the time— the more valuable the treasure.

Four years later, he developed an additional heart issue that required him to undergo his fifth and sixth open-heart surgeries— within the same week! I had never even heard of a person having two open-heart surgeries in the same week. Five years later, Colton had to have another valve replacement, but thankfully, this procedure did not require another open-heart surgery. Three years after that, we had another cancer scare with Anna Grace that ultimately turned out to be nothing of concern. Two years later, Colton had to be taken to the hospital by ambulance twice due to some serious heart rhythm issues in which his heart rate was over 250 beats per minute. And a few years later, I had a near-fatal heart attack and required five cardiac stents. Two months after that, I was diagnosed with two brain aneurysms.

Of all the adversity that we have faced during our decades-long season of storms, our experience has been consistent. The Lord did not just bring us *to the storms*—He brought us *through the storms*! And He will do the same for you. How do I know that? Because God's Word declares it.

→ Psalm 46:1: "God is our refuge and strength, an ever-present help in trouble."

→ Psalm 34:7: "The angel of the Lord encamps around those who fear him, and he delivers them."

→ Psalm 34:17-18: "The righteous cry out, and the Lord hears them; he delivers them from all their troubles."

It helps to remember that we are not just reading Bible verses; we are receiving a message from the Lord. What is His message to you? God is *your* refuge and *your* source of strength. He is the One you should run to for shelter from life's storms and the One who empowers you to persevere. He is always right there with *you* in times of trouble. The presence of the Lord sets up camp all around *your* life, and He delivers *you*. When *you* cry out to God, He *hears you,* and He *delivers you* from all of your troubles. As you trust the Lord in your storms, He will empower you to stand strong, win the battle, and march forward into your God-given destiny.

REFLECTION & APPLICATION

1) What resistance have you faced that God used in your life to increase your strength?

2) Did you identify a person that you greatly admire? If so, perhaps you would consider contacting that person to tell them what an inspiration they have been to you. You might also ask them for advice on navigating tough times.

SAMPLE PRAYER

Lord, please help me to remember that Your Word teaches us to expect and prepare for adversity. Jesus, You told us that in this world, we would experience trouble, but we should be encouraged by the fact that You have overcome the world. And because I am a child of God, I am more than a conqueror through Christ. When I face adversity, help me to reject the idea that "this should not be happening to me" and embrace the truth that if I stay focused on You and trust You in my storm, You will bring me through to victory.

FAITH DECLARATION

Lord, I declare by faith that I will grow stronger and more mature in my faith because I choose to trust You in times of trouble rather than blaming You. I choose to view resistance as an opportunity to build the strong character of Christ in my life. And I confess that You are always with me—in the good times and the bad times. You will never leave me nor forsake me, and I choose to celebrate Your consistent presence in my life.

SCRIPTURE FOR THE STORM

"Consider it pure joy, my brothers and sisters, whenever you face trials of many kinds because you know that the testing of your faith produces perseverance. Let perseverance finish its work so that you may be mature and complete, not lacking anything."

—James 1:2-4

CHAPTER 5

UNDER HIS FEET

"Shortly before dawn Jesus went out to them, walking on the lake."
—Matthew 14:25

N ow we come to a spectacular part of this story. This verse gives us a clue as to how long the disciples had been struggling against the storm. Jesus approached them "shortly before dawn." This means that they had likely been in a fight for survival for eight to ten hours. Just in time, Jesus came to the aid of His exhausted, fearful, and struggling disciples—*walking on the water*! This was no doubt the first such occurrence ever witnessed on this planet. A few thoughts immediately come to mind regarding this shocking suspension of the physical laws of nature.

First, nothing can stop the Lord from coming to the aid of His people. As the disciples were no doubt beginning to wonder how they could even survive the storm, God did what God does. He made a way where there was no way. The life of Jesus is a seminar on the subject of making impossible things possible. When people had exhausted all known options and still could not find healing, Jesus made a way.

When the sisters of Lazarus mourned the premature death of their beloved brother and longed to see him again, Jesus made a way. When towns were terrorized by demon-possessed men that no one could control, Jesus made a way. And, finally, when there appeared to be no way for mankind to ever be truly reconciled to God, Jesus made a way!

Secondly, the greatest danger to the disciples in this storm was the crashing waves that threatened to capsize their boat and drown them in the depths. Storm winds can be frightening, but as long as the boat stays afloat, those winds are not deadly. Crashing waves can be terrifying, but if the boat doesn't sink, those waves are not deadly. I believe there is much treasure that the Scriptures hold for us that we have yet to recognize. One such treasure is this truth: When Jesus came to them, He was . . . WALKING ON THEIR PROBLEM!

> When Jesus came to them, He was
> . . . WALKING ON THEIR PROBLEM!

Everything that frightens us and everything that threatens us is . . . UNDER HIS FEET!

I believe this is one of the reasons the Lord sent them into the storm in the first place. He wanted them to know that He could not only calm their stormy circumstances when He was already in the boat, but He could literally walk on anything that threatened them!

Earlier, we mentioned other times in the Bible when God allowed His people to get into situations that seemed impossible to escape. They did not enjoy those trials and would not have chosen to go through them. But the fact is that if the people of Israel had never had their backs against the Red Sea, they would never have discovered that God can part the waters. If Shadrach, Meshach, and Abednego had not been thrown into the fiery furnace, they would never have known that God can rescue His people from the flames.

And as much as we hate going through hard times, we would never be able to comprehend the lengths to which God will go in order to rescue us if we never face the threatening storms of life. If we can maintain a healthy attitude and perspective, every fiery trial we overcome can strengthen our faith and trust in God. Every crisis that we will ever face in life is *under His feet*. When referring to Jesus, First Corinthians 15:27 (BSB) states that "God has [placed] all things under his feet."

Consider the following references:

→ Ephesians 1:22: "And God placed all things under his feet and appointed him to be head over everything for the church."

→ Matthew 28:18: "Then Jesus came to them and said, 'All authority in heaven and on earth has been given to me.'"

As with so many verses in Scripture, this verse contains a powerful nugget of truth that is hidden from us as we read the English translation. The word "authority" in this verse is a translation of the Greek word *exousia*. The depth of its meaning goes beyond a simple understanding of declared authority. The word here carries the meaning of having "authority to take action." It is not just about title or position; it implies energetic action exercised by the one in authority in accordance with His own will.

There are many other verses in the Scriptures that clearly declare the authority that resides in Christ. There are several references in the gospels that align with this truth. Matthew 22:44, Mark 12:36, and Luke 20:42-43 all quote the following verse found in Psalm 110:1:

"The Lord says to my Lord: 'Sit at my right hand until I make your enemies a footstool for your feet.'" According to Jesus' interpretation of this verse in the Gospels, this is obviously a reference to the Son of God in heaven sitting at the right hand of the throne of God. So, the above-referenced verses from the Gospels are not the earliest references to the power and authority that places everything under the feet of Christ because these verses reference a psalm of David that prophetically declares the same principle.

However, the Psalm of David is not the earliest reference to this principle either. Barely three pages into the book of Genesis, after Adam and Eve sinned, we find God passing judgment on the serpent, and in Genesis 3:15, God prophetically refers to the seed of the woman. This is a reference to the coming Messiah of Israel and God declares to the serpent, "You will bruise his heel, but he will crush your head" (author paraphrase). From the very beginning, everything in the universe—including the forces of darkness—has been placed *under the feet of Jesus.* Every force of evil is under His feet. Everything that threatens you is under His feet.

> Everything that frightens you and attacks you is under His feet.

As a child of God, there is nothing in our lives that Jesus can't defeat! He can walk all over the things that try to overwhelm us. We need to be encouraged that no matter what sin, what weakness, what addiction or what temptation comes against us—our Lord can come to us and demonstrate that anything we face is under His feet, and He will set us free! As we can see, the Bible makes it very clear that Jesus has been given all authority to rule. When we find ourselves facing a storm in life, we need to remember that even though we can't control all the aspects of the trial, our Lord is fully capable of walking all over anything that threatens us!

What storm are you facing? No matter what it is, you can take comfort in the fact that the things that frighten us don't frighten the Lord. He has the authority, and He has a plan to bring you through it! When we read about all of the troubled times that God's people have overcome, it should encourage us to realize that God did not just bring them to it; He brought them through it! The same is true for us. He doesn't just bring us to it; He brings us through it!

> What storm are you facing? No matter what it is, you can take comfort in the fact that the things that frighten us don't frighten the Lord.

Have you ever faced a trial in life that you honestly did not think you would survive? Take a minute to consider something. What I'm about to say, on the surface, may seem so obvious that it borders on the absurd. But indulge me for a moment, and try to look beyond the surface. The fact that you are reading this book indicates a number of different things. One of the most basic things it indicates is that you are alive and well.

Why would I take the time to point out something so obvious? Because sometimes, in life our focus on our problems can lead us to overlook the blessings that are right in front of us. Let me clarify my reason for pointing out the undeniable fact of your continued existence. The Bible declares that our enemy has a goal to steal, kill, and destroy. And every strategy that the enemy has employed to try to destroy you up to this very moment—has failed! You are still here! You are not dead. You are not destroyed. You may have been injured, and you may have sustained some damage, but you are still here! You are still standing. It is easy for us to ruminate on all the bad stuff that has happened to us. But if we look at the big picture, we will realize that nothing that we have endured has been able to stop us from living life. We Are Still Here!!

Through the years, as I have proclaimed this truth, I have witnessed a profound change in people's countenance as it suddenly dawned on them that in spite of everything they had endured, the simple fact of their continued existence was unmistakable evidence of their victory over all of the strategies that Hell had deployed to destroy their lives. It totally changes our perspective when we view life this way. It also bolsters our confidence as we are reminded that Jesus has been given unrestricted authority over everything in our life. And everything that can come as a threat against us is under His feet.

Understanding these truths does not exempt us from future challenges. There will always be threats to face. But the next time you face a raging storm in life, lift your gaze, and you will see that your Lord is coming to you, treading on your trouble as He takes authority over it to rescue you.

REFLECTION & APPLICATION

1) Can you describe a time when the Lord appeared in your storm and demonstrated full authority over your situation?

2) Make a list of all the major attacks that Satan has employed to destroy your life. At the top of that list, add the title "The Devil's Failed Attempts." Every strategy that Satan has used to take you out of this world has failed. You are still here—and so is your divine destiny!

3) What is the most important lesson that God has taught you as you've endured the storms of life?

SAMPLE PRAYER

Lord, I acknowledge and celebrate the fact that every attack the devil has launched against me to destroy my life has failed. I am still here because You have rescued me and strengthened me through the seasons of adversity. I pray that You will continue to demonstrate that everything that frightens me and everything that threatens me is under Your feet. There is no evil in this world that You can't stomp all over, and I pray that You will continue to stamp out the devil's threats by Your mighty power. I pray these things in the mighty name of Jesus! Amen.

FAITH DECLARATION

Lord, I declare by faith that every attack I will ever encounter is firmly under Your feet. You can walk all over anything that comes against me. I acknowledge Your authority over the universe, and I willingly submit to Your authority in my life. I declare that not only have Satan's attempts to destroy my life failed in the past, but they will also fail in the future. I declare these things by faith in the name of Jesus! Amen.

CHAPTER 6

THE INNER STORM

*"When the disciples saw him walking on the lake, they were
terrified. 'It's a ghost,' they said, and cried out in fear."*
—Matthew 14:26

When the disciples saw Jesus walking on the lake, they were terrified and thought that they were seeing a ghost. No doubt, the fear that they felt in that moment only added to the level of terror they were already experiencing as they struggled to survive in the storm. In that moment, they were totally convinced that they were seeing a ghost—and they were totally wrong. When we find ourselves in the middle of a crisis, our thoughts can run wild, and if we do not control them, they can lead us to all sorts of incorrect assumptions and mistaken conclusions.

> When we find ourselves in the middle of a crisis, our thoughts can run wild, and if we do not control them, they can lead us to all sorts of incorrect assumptions and mistaken conclusions.

One example that is seared into my memory is a time when Anna Grace was still in active treatment at St. Jude and was having an MRI of her brain. She would have scans periodically to look for any changes in brain structure and to make sure there was no tumor growing back. Nancy and I did our best to keep a positive outlook, but the truth is that any parent in our situation would have a bit of trepidation about the scans.

On one occasion, we were in the waiting room while Anna was in the MRI, and it was about time for her to be finished. We saw her anesthesiologist walking down the hall and knew that the scan was done. He came over, and we asked how things had gone. He replied, "Well, the anesthesia went fine" (emphasis on the word "anesthesia"). The way he said it made it sound like the other aspects of the test hadn't gone so well. They called us back to get Anna, and we took her home, knowing that we would have to wait until the next day to get the official report from her test.

That night was torture. We prayed and fought against worry all night long. Our thoughts were ravaged by every possible bad report, and we didn't sleep much at all. The next day, we went back for her daily appointment, and finally, the report came back: no tumor—no problems! We were relieved on a level that is hard to describe. We told her doctor about the anesthesiologist's comment and lamented the fact that we had spent a miserable night for no reason.

In times of trouble, there will always be ample opportunity for our thoughts to run wild and lead us in the wrong direction. The most challenging struggles we face in life can often occur in our minds. That doesn't mean that the battles are not real; it just means that they occur in the invisible realm of our thoughts and emotions. In physical storms, we can't actually see the wind, but we can easily identify its destructive effects. In mental and spiritual warfare, we can't actually see the enemy's attacks, but we can easily identify their destructive effects.

Thankfully, God's Word provides wisdom and understanding that we desperately need in order to fend off the onslaughts of Satan. Second Corinthians 2:11 provides valuable insight to help us fight these battles "in order that Satan might not outwit us. For we are not unaware of his schemes." The word "schemes" in this verse comes from the Greek word *noema* which means "a thought or purpose." But this word is also used to convey the idea of "a design, the mind, the heart, the soul and feelings." I believe this word reveals to us that Satan's schemes against us are aimed at our mind, our heart, our soul, and our emotions.

There are many other places in the Bible that confirm the devil's strategy to fill our minds with poisonous thoughts, false beliefs, confusion, anger, depression, anxiety, and fear. He also uses lying emotions to try to implant feelings of doom and gloom, even when our circumstances would not indicate such things. Have you ever had a thought run through your mind that was so strange that you immediately wondered, *Where in the world did that come from?* If you are human, the answer is probably yes. If we monitor our thoughts, it doesn't take long to realize that everything that *pops into your head* did not originate there. The majority of our thoughts probably do develop in our own minds, but thoughts and ideas can also come from other people, from God, or from the devil.

That is one reason that the Word of God gives us some practical instruction on this topic. In 2 Corinthians 10:5, the Word instructs us to "take captive every thought to make it obedient to Christ." Our family has repeatedly learned the value of guarding our thoughts and monitoring our mindset. We have been given not only the right but also the responsibility to take control of our thoughts and to not let them lead us astray. This is always important, but it is even more critical to survive the storms of life.

> Do not let your thoughts and emotions dictate to you. Take authority over them to bring them into alignment with the truth of God's Word, and you can not only survive in the storm, but you can also thrive in the storm!

Do not let your thoughts and emotions dictate to you. Take authority over them to bring them into alignment with the truth of God's Word, and you can not only survive in the storm, but you can also thrive in the storm! If we drill down into the text of 2 Corinthians 10:4-5, we find an interesting sequence of verbs that are very revealing:

> *For the weapons of our warfare are not carnal but mighty in God for pulling down strongholds, casting down arguments and*

every high thing that exalts itself against the knowledge of God,
bringing every thought into captivity to the obedience of Christ.
—2 Corinthians 10:4-5 (NKJV)

Years ago, while writing in my devotional journal after reading this text, I noticed something about the verbs that piqued my interest. There is a distinct increase in intensity that is required as the process moves from thoughts to arguments and then to strongholds. The apostle Paul lists the sequence from most difficult to least difficult, but for our purposes, we will view them in the reverse order.

THOUGHTS

Everything begins with a thought. You are reading this book because at some point, you thought, *I think I'll get a book about how to make it through times of trouble.* Everywhere we go and everything we do— those actions begin in our thought processes. Because of this, if we need to make a change in our life, that change first has to take place in our thought life. In the above verses, Paul uses the phrase "take captive every thought."

Remember that these verses were written in the context of warfare, so the verb in the original Greek describes the image of a soldier who has already captured and bound his enemy and is leading him away with the point of his spear sticking into the back of his prisoner. This indicates that in mental battles and spiritual warfare, stopping an enemy attack at the thought level—*before it gets firmly implanted*— represents the lowest level of challenge and the easiest victory in the battle of the mind. This concept aligns with many other commonsense principles of life. Dealing with problems as soon as they appear always makes the solution easier and more effective than allowing situations to grow worse and get out of control.

ARGUMENTS

So, what happens if we fail to take authority and exercise control of a thought? That single thought becomes a series of related thoughts on which we ruminate as we attempt to clarify and construct the idea in our mind. The word within this context means "a reasoning that is hostile toward our faith in Christ." Such a reasoning can then become an argument against the Word of God and the work of God in us. It is interesting to note that the word translated as "argument" in this verse is the Greek word *logismos*. This is actually the root of the English terms "logic" and "logical." Many times, when Satan tries to construct an argument in our minds against the things of God, he is skilled at making his argument sound logical. At this level of warfare, a more intense response is required. Here, Paul uses the phrase "casting down arguments and every high thing that exalts itself against the knowledge of God."

Notice the uptick in intensity? If we intervene at the *thought* level, we need only to *take it captive*. If we allow the thought to gain momentum and become a reasoning or as some translations call it, an imagination then, we have to "cast it down." The image of casting something down definitely indicates more of a struggle than simply "taking it captive." So, if we wait until something becomes a reasoning, argument, or imagination, we will have a more difficult time dealing with it.

STRONGHOLDS

We have discussed what happens if we allow a thought to continue to develop unmonitored and unchecked. It can grow into an argument against God's agenda for our life. What happens if we still do not intervene at the argument level? It will continue to develop until it becomes a stronghold in our life. The word here means a "fortress" which is a place that is heavily fortified and easily defended from attack. Paul wrote these words to the church at Corinth, and they would have definitely related to the imagery of a stronghold because there was a high hill overlooking ancient Corinth, and on top of that hill was a fortress.

Remember that the context for all of this is spiritual warfare. If we stand by and allow an enemy stronghold to be constructed in our territory, it can be used as a base of operations from which attacks can be launched against us. If, early in the process, we "take captive every thought" that is not in obedience to Christ, that is the lowest level of conflict and the easiest victory to win. If we allow things to progress to the argument level, we have to "cast it down" which requires more energy and effort to accomplish. Finally, if we let things progress to the level of a stronghold, even more effort is required.

Paul uses the phrase "pulling down strongholds" to describe the difficulty of this task. Think with me for a moment about the literal meaning of the words here. When you have to pull something down, where is it? It is over you and above you. Simply put, you can't pull something down if it is already below you; that would be pushing it down. The very act of pulling down requires that whatever it is that you are pulling down is above you.

Why is this significant? Because, by definition, a stronghold in our life is something that controls us, not the other way around. When something reaches the level of a stronghold, it is extremely difficult to eliminate. Every sort of addiction ranging from drugs and alcohol to pornography to gambling could all be classified as a spiritual stronghold. People also deal with strongholds of fear, anxiety, depression, and many other oppressions. We must not ever allow the enemy to build a stronghold in our lives because if we do, major warfare will be required for us to gain our freedom. It is always important for us to monitor our thought life to avoid this negative progression that leads us to future battles, but it is also vital that we take authority over our thoughts when we are already in a crisis.

> We must not ever allow the enemy to build a stronghold in our lives because if we do, major warfare will be required for us to gain our freedom.

Speaking of crisis, let's rejoin the disciples back on the storm-tossed sea as they were fighting for survival. As we already stated, when the disciples saw Jesus, they did not immediately recognize Him. There could be a number of reasons for this. Clearly, they were intensely focused on trying to navigate the storm, and that demanded all of their attention. It was also before dawn, so it was likely still somewhat dark. And the violent winds were no doubt blowing mist and water against them. All of these elements in combination could easily explain their lack of recognition.

I believe there is another valuable lesson in this part of the story for all of us. We have already mentioned the fact that the Lord has promised to always be with us, but it is equally true that there may be times during our seasons of adversity when we do not immediately recognize His presence. When all of our attention is focused on trying to survive the storm, we may fail to realize that the Lord is still present with us in the middle of our struggle.

As you already know, Nancy and I have faced this challenge more times than we ever expected. When you are in a fight for survival, it can be very easy to feel abandoned and all alone in your troubles. Sometimes, when you see direct evidence that God is working in your circumstances, it can still be less encouraging than you might expect. One prominent example that comes to mind is when Anna Grace was diagnosed with cancer. You may remember from the chapter about Anna Grace the overwhelming and undeniable evidence that God orchestrated our entire adoption process to guarantee that we would be matched up with her. That decision was essentially in the hands of the Chinese government, and we had no input in the matter.

As I mentioned in the earlier chapter, it was simultaneously comforting and frustrating to recognize God's involvement at such an obvious level. It was comforting because we knew that God was guiding the process; it was frustrating because we could not help wondering why God didn't just heal her of the cancer since He was clearly active in everything that happened. The Lord went to all the trouble to guide every aspect of the process to ensure that she would be adopted by a family that was already "trained" to handle adversity. And that family just so happened to live twenty minutes from the number one children's cancer research hospital in the world.

If He went to all that trouble, why not just heal her instantly? It certainly sounded like a valid question to us. There will always be an abundance of questions in the middle of your storms. But you cannot afford to allow yourself to get "stuck" in your questions. We will all have unanswered questions about things we don't understand. How we choose to respond to those questions will have a greater impact on our lives than the actual events that inspired them.

Have you ever gotten stuck on a question while taking an exam? The proper strategy in that scenario is to skip that question and keep moving through the exam. One reason this approach is effective is because if you keep progressing through the test, you may come across information later in the test that helps you answer the question you had to skip. Another reason to keep moving is so that you can complete the rest of the questions that you can answer. It wouldn't make sense to fail the whole test because you got stuck on one question you couldn't answer. This principle not only works in formal education—it works in life.

Sometimes you may recognize the Lord in the middle of your storm, and sometimes, you may not. That brings me to an interesting thought I had in reading the next verses in Matthew 14. As I was reading this story one day and trying to visualize what the disciples were experiencing, something occurred to me that I had never considered. The water that Jesus was walking on was not a smooth glassy surface. It was a turbulent sea of rolling waves.

In light of that, could it be possible that Jesus was actually walking up and down the waves as one would traverse up one side of a hill and down the other side as He made His way out to the disciples? If so, could it be that as He crested the top of a wave, He was visible to them for a moment? And as He descended down the other side of the wave, He temporarily disappeared from their view? If this was the case, they would have had a "now you see me, now you don't" experience as Jesus made His way toward them.

> I don't know about you, but I have had many "now you see me, now you don't" experiences throughout all the storms that we have faced.

I don't know about you, but I have had many "now you see me, now you don't" experiences throughout all the storms that we have faced. Sometimes, it was obvious that the Lord was right there. Other times, I wondered if He were anywhere near us in our crisis. Have you ever felt that way? Those of us who have are not alone. Psalm 10:1 (ESV) confirms this experience: "Why, O Lord, do you stand far away? Why do you hide yourself in times of trouble?" Most scholars believe that chronologically the oldest book in the Bible is the book of Job. I think it is significant that the very first Holy Spirit-inspired scriptures address the issue of unanswered questions that we all face in life.

If you are struggling with things you don't understand, it is certainly okay to be honest about it. God knows anyway. What I glean from this part of the story is a very important principle that can help to prepare us for tough times and keep us encouraged in our storms. The principle is this: sometimes, we can see the Lord in our storms, and sometimes, we can't. However, He has promised to always be with us, whether we can see Him or not. And we must choose to stand in faith and lean on that promise—not on our own understanding.

When the disciples cried out in fear and declared that they were seeing a ghost, they were totally convinced that their perceptions and opinions were correct. The record of this event does not indicate any doubt on their part that they were seeing a ghost. Their experience likely aligns with experiences that we all have had when we were totally convinced of something that turned out to be false. We can use the principles of this chapter to help us filter out the false impressions that develop in our own minds or are planted by the enemy of our soul. God's Word equips us to navigate the inward storms of our thoughts and emotions.

REFLECTION & APPLICATION

1) Describe a time of crisis in your life when you wondered if God was even aware of your situation.

2) Describe a time of crisis in your life when God's presence was obvious in your situation.

3) How can you apply the principles in this chapter to help you monitor your thought life and defend against Satan's implanted thoughts and emotions?

4) How can you apply the principles of this chapter to deal with your unanswered questions?

SAMPLE PRAYER

Lord, I pray that You will help me to be alert and filter every thought through the Word of God to make sure that it lines up with Your eternal truth and not just the temporary logic of this world. Help me to have my mind renewed daily as I invest time in worship, prayer, and Your Word. Please empower me with Your Holy Spirit to take captive every thought, cast down every argument against Your kingdom, and pull down any stronghold that the enemy is trying to construct in my life. I pray these things in the mighty name of Jesus! Amen.

FAITH DECLARATION

Lord, I declare by faith that I will consistently monitor what is going on in my mind to make sure that my thoughts are in alignment with Your Word. By faith, I take captive every thought, cast down every argument that rises up against You, and pull down any stronghold of the enemy in my life. I choose to lean on Your eternal truth and not my limited understanding. I declare these things by faith in the name of Jesus!

CHAPTER 7

A WORD FROM THE LORD

"But Jesus immediately said to them: 'Take courage! It is I. Don't be afraid.'"
—Matthew 14:27

This verse represents the first time that the disciples had heard a word from the Lord since His initial instruction that sent them into the storm. It followed right after they had failed to recognize Him and thought that He was a ghost. Immediately, Jesus spoke into their storm a word of instruction and assurance.

DON'T BE AFRAID

He began with the first phase of a two-part instruction: "Take courage!" Of course, in our modern-day vernacular, we don't really use the phrase "take courage." We tend to lean more toward the second phrase of Jesus' instruction in which He said, "Don't be afraid." These two facets of Jesus' message to His disciples are obviously related in their purpose to deal with the fear that the disciples were experiencing. It is interesting to note that the phrase "do not be afraid" was the standard greeting in virtually every scriptural account when an angel brought a message from God. It is as if the Lord were emphasizing that message by its repetition. In certain translations of the Bible, the phrase "do not be afraid" appears up to 366 times. That's one for every day of the year—plus one extra for leap year!

Next, Jesus provided His disciples with the reason that they should not be afraid. He positively identified Himself to His terrified disciples with the phrase "It is I." Of course, Jesus was assuring the disciples that He was not a water-walking ghost, but there is more beneath the surface waiting to be discovered. The phrase "It is I" is a translation of the original Greek text that reads, *ego eimi*. This is a phrase that is used in some of the most significant passages in the entire New Testament. *Ego eimi* is also translated into English as "I Am."

You may remember the seven "I Am" statements of Christ.

→ I am the bread of life. (John 6:35, 41, 48, 51)

→ I am the light of the world. (John 8:12)

→ I am the door of the sheep. (John 10:7, 9)

→ I am the resurrection and the life. (John 11:25)

→ I am the good shepherd. (John 10:11, 14)

→ I am the way, the truth, and the life. (John 14:6)

→ I am the true vine. (John 15:1, 5)

THE GREAT I Am

These are some of the most celebrated and beloved verses in the entire New Testament. And in every single case, the phrase "I Am" in English comes from the words *ego eimi* in Greek. Why is that significant? Because every time Jesus used the phrase "I Am," His Jewish listeners would immediately be reminded of the passage in the Old Testament that details the account of Moses hearing God speak to him from the middle of a burning bush. In Exodus 3, God spoke to Moses and called him to return to Egypt and tell Pharaoh to let the Israelites go free:

> But Moses said to God, "Who am I that I should go to Pharaoh and bring the Israelites out of Egypt?"
>
> And God said, "I will be with you. And this will be the sign to you that it is I who have sent you: When you have brought the people out of Egypt, you will worship God on this mountain."
>
> Moses said to God, "Suppose I go to the Israelites and say to them, 'The God of your fathers has sent me to you,' and they ask me, 'What is his name?' Then what shall I tell them?"
>
> God said to Moses, "I Am who I Am. This is what you are to say to the Israelites: 'I Am has sent me to you.'" —Exodus 3:11-14

Every time Jesus used the phrase "I Am," His Jewish listeners would immediately be reminded of the passage in the Old Testament that details the account of Moses hearing God speak to him from the middle of a burning bush.

Ever since God delivered the children of Israel from Egyptian bondage, the phrase "I Am" has been linked to God Himself. One of the reasons that the Pharisees hated Jesus so much was because every time He made one of the "I Am" statements, they realized that He was claiming to be God's Messiah.

This reveals a whole new dimension of Jesus' message to His disciples. He was not simply identifying Himself. He was simultaneously declaring and demonstrating that He was indeed God's Messiah by invoking the phrase "I AM" while walking on the stormy seas. Only God Himself could override the laws of nature in such a manner as He was displaying at that moment, as well as earlier in the day when He multiplied the loaves and fish to feed thousands of people.

Can you imagine how comforting it was for the disciples to receive a "word" from the Lord in the middle of their storm? Just the confirmation that He was aware and engaged in their situation before they could see Him must have been incredibly encouraging. I can tell you from personal experience that if there's anything you are going to need in a time of storm, it is a word from the Lord.

THE BENEFITS OF THE WORD

The primary method that God uses to speak to us is through His Word. I could not even begin to calculate all the times in my life when I desperately needed guidance, encouragement, or instruction. And in so many of those times, I would feel the Lord's leading to what I thought was a random passage of scripture, only to find out that it was exactly what I needed to hear in that moment. My sense of awe in that fact is punctuated by the number of times I have gone back to review an old devotional journal and seen this testimony in my own handwriting.

This is yet another reason that I am such an advocate of journaling as a part of one's spiritual process. To be able to go back and read my own testimony of what I sensed the Lord speaking to me, both in the good times and in the bad, has been one of the most incredible blessings of my life! So many times, especially as we get older, we can feel a sense that our life seems to be slipping away quickly. But every word I have written in my devotional journals over the last thirty-plus years has preserved a portion of my life that I can go back and relive, and in some cases, relearn vital lessons from the past.

So many times, those words from the Lord were just what I needed to carry me through the toughest days in my life. Countless volumes have been written dissecting, explaining, and celebrating the Bible. So, it would be impossible to deal with this subject in an exhaustive way, but there are a few nuggets of truth that I would like to highlight in a general sense. The longest chapter in the Bible is Psalm 119. It contains 176 verses. And virtually every one of those verses is a celebration of God's Word. Here are a few of my favorites:

→ Psalm 119:11: "I have hidden your word in my heart that I might not sin against you."

→ Psalm 119:18: "Open my eyes that I may see wonderful things in your law."

→ Psalm 119:37: "Turn my eyes away from worthless things; preserve my life according to your word."

→ Psalm 119:105: "Your word is a lamp for my feet, a light on my path."

There is so much truth in just this single chapter that one could spend weeks in study and not exhaust the material. We discover powerful truths even if we just condense the previous verses into a single thought. In verse 11, we learn that proactively engaging and interacting with God's Word strengthens us spiritually and helps us avoid sinful behavior. In verse 18, we see that God has buried great treasures of truth in His Word, and we need His help to dig them out. In verse 37, our tendency towards squandering our attention on things of little value is remedied as we focus on the Word, and in doing so, our life is preserved. And finally, in verse 105 (my personal favorite), God's Word speaks of itself and describes some of its most important functions. His Word is a lamp for my feet and a light for my path. It shows me where I am, and it shows me where I'm going. It reveals my *position,* and it illuminates my *path*.

This is true on so many levels. How many times has God's Word revealed something in our lives of which we were previously unaware? The Word shines a light on our position and shows us where we stand with God. Beyond that, it also highlights that path that we have chosen to walk and shows us where we will end up if we stay on that path.

The disciples desperately needed a word from the Lord during their storm, and they benefitted greatly when they received it. The same is true with us. One of the most important things any of us can do in seasons of trouble is to spend a significant amount of time in God's presence and remain focused on Him instead of our problems. Receiving a word from the Lord will be vital to your ability to withstand the storms of life!

> Receiving a word from the Lord will be vital to your ability to withstand the storms of life!

THOROUGHLY EQUIPPED FOR THE VOYAGE

The verses we reviewed from Psalm 119 reveal powerful benefits that we receive as we focus on God's Word. There are numerous other places in the Bible that declare the positive impact of scripture on our lives. One of the most prominent of those texts is found in 2 Timothy 3:16-17:

All scripture is God-breathed and is useful for teaching, rebuking, correcting and training in righteousness, so that the man of God may be thoroughly equipped for every good work.

These are some of the key verses in the New Testament and most Christians have heard sermons based on them.

Most teaching on this passage focuses heavily on verse 16, and there is certainly nothing wrong with that because that verse affirms that the Scriptures are inspired by God and are essential to the process of discipleship. But there is a powerful truth that is often overlooked in the following verse: "So that the man of God may be thoroughly equipped for every good work." This verse reveals the overarching purpose of the individual functions of the Scriptures, and it does so in a way that aligns perfectly with the theme of this book.

The phrase "thoroughly equipped" comes from the Greek word *exartizo* which means to "completely equip, to totally deck out and fully furnish." Bible scholars indicate that this word was used to describe a ship that had formerly been ill-equipped for a long journey. But then the owner of the ship *decked it out* until it was thoroughly prepared with the equipment and supplies that would be needed for it to sail anywhere on long voyages—even through the occasional turbulence of stormy seas. I believe that Paul is using this image to teach us that we are not prepared to navigate through life until we have been thoroughly equipped with the Word of God.

The word that Jesus spoke to His disciples in that stormy sea had an immediate effect. It corrected their false perception that they were looking at a ghost and showed them that they were not alone in their storm because Jesus was present with them. As we prayed and sought the Lord, God was faithful to speak a word to us in every storm we faced. Without those words of encouragement, assurance, and guidance, I don't believe we would have made it through all the tough times. But God's Word thoroughly equipped us with everything we needed to withstand the wind and the waves that were crashing against our lives. *To navigate this life, you will need to be thoroughly equipped.* So, I encourage you to invest significant time in the Word of God because that is the process that God has ordained to equip us for the voyage of life.

REFLECTION & APPLICATION

1) Describe a time when you desperately needed a word from the Lord?

2) When have you received a much-needed word from God that impacted your life in a powerful way?

3) Typically, a ship is furnished with the equipment and supplies for a long journey before it leaves the harbor. This relates to our lives. It is always a wise choice to be thoroughly equipped by spending time in God's Word before we leave the safety of the harbor. How can you improve your daily devotional life so that you will be ready for whatever you encounter on your journey of life?

SAMPLE PRAYER

Lord, I thank You for the abundant provisions for the voyage of life that are available to me through Your Word. Please help me not to be distracted by the trivial things in life. I want to focus on spending time with You in Your Word so that I can be thoroughly equipped for every good work that You have in store for me. When the winds of adversity blow against my life, help me to look to You for a Word to guide and sustain me. In Jesus' name, I pray. Amen!

FAITH DECLARATION

Lord, I declare by faith that every provision that I will need for life's journey will be provided by You as I spend time in Your Word. I declare that every benefit of filling my mind with Your Word will come to full fruition. I also declare by faith that as I immerse myself in Your presence and in Your Word, I will receive everything that I need to sustain me through the voyage of life. I will not wait until the storm hits to seek a word from You; I will invest my time and energy in Your Word before I leave the safety of the harbor. I declare these things by faith in the name of Jesus!

CHAPTER 8
THE CERTAINTY OF UNCERTAINTY

"But Jesus immediately said to them: 'Take courage!
It is I. Don't be afraid.' 'Lord, if it's you,' Peter
replied, 'tell me to come to you on the water.'"
—Matthew 14:27-28

Even after Jesus had spoken words of encouragement to the disciples and positively identified Himself, Peter spoke up and said, "Lord, if it's you...." When I read these verses from the comfort of my recliner, my first response was, "Really, Peter—if ?" Jesus had just positively identified Himself and told His disciples not to be afraid. It's easy for us to judge others (including biblical characters) in their times of struggle. But we should also remember that even though Jesus had spoken an encouraging word to them, they were *still engulfed in the chaos* of the storm. I chose the title of this chapter based on the fact that the struggle with uncertainty is universal. We all know what it's like to struggle with doubts and confusion—especially at times when we are being battered by the storms of life. There have been many times that I have struggled to recognize the Lord's presence when I was facing a swirling cyclone of crisis.

> We all know what it's like to struggle with doubts and confusion—especially at times when we are being battered by the storms of life.

At the time of this writing, we are all living in the most intense season of uncertainty in our lifetime. The atmosphere of chaos in our society is the result of several different factors: increasing natural disasters, large-scale cultural shifts, growing political polarization, and racial tension—all taking place during a pandemic such as the world has not witnessed in the last one hundred years. Fortunately, God has not left us helpless or hopeless. His Word is filled with relevant and practical principles to help us navigate the seasons of uncertainty that we will all face in life.

So often, in times of trouble, the enemy of our soul attempts to add condemnation to the load that we are already carrying. Feeling condemned for struggling with uncertainty is a very common experience among followers of Christ. But it is also very encouraging when we realize that virtually every prominent character in the Bible struggled with seasons of uncertainty.

POTENTIAL SOURCES OF UNCERTAINTY
Unmet Expectations and Confusing Circumstances
After baptizing Jesus, John the Baptist publicly declared in John 1:29 that Jesus was the "Lamb of God who takes away the sin of the world." But Luke 7 records that later, John sent messengers to ask Jesus if He was actually the Messiah. What happened to cause John

to have doubts? He was in the middle of an intense storm in his life. He had been sitting in prison for about a year and likely knew that he was going to be executed. I'm sure that is not what he expected when he declared Jesus to be the "Lamb of God."

Since John was chosen by God to be the forerunner of Christ, I imagine that he expected to be a continuing part of the kingdom that Jesus had come to establish. But sitting in prison awaiting execution doesn't line up very well with that expectation. When crisis strikes and our vision of the future is threatened, we tend to wrestle with doubts and uncertainties because we don't understand what is happening. John the Baptist experienced some of the main catalysts that can trigger uncertainty—unmet expectations and confusing circumstances.

It is unlikely that you are sitting in prison awaiting execution for faithfully preaching the gospel. But I imagine that you can relate to the disappointment of unmet expectations. When God allows a crisis to develop in our lives in spite of our obedience to His will, it can be very confusing and difficult to process.

Scott, a man in our church family, was on the way home from work one evening during a thunderstorm. As he was driving on the highway, he witnessed a car accident and pulled over to check on the victims. He had received extensive medical training in the military and was assisting a woman and her four-year-old child who were injured in the crash. He literally saved their lives, but in the process of getting them safely out of their vehicle and off the road, another car crashed into their vehicle which then ran over Scott.

He suffered many broken bones, severe internal injuries, and a near-fatal traumatic brain injury. He spent months in the hospital, underwent dozens of surgeries, and has been in rehab for over four years. At this point, he is still unable to walk unassisted, has difficulty speaking clearly, and requires around-the-clock care. It was a very confusing situation for Scott's family and friends to process the fact that the victims he rescued returned to normal life quickly while the person who rescued them is still living in the chaos of this storm.

Struggles with uncertainty can be caused by unmet expectations and confusing circumstances.

Watching a Loved One Suffer

There is a story in Mark 9 about a father who brought his son to Jesus' disciples to be healed. The boy was being attacked by an evil spirit that manifested by taking away his ability to speak and causing him to suffer convulsions. The disciples were unable to cast out the evil spirit, and when Jesus arrived, He asked about the situation and spoke to the boy's father who said:

> *"If you can do anything, please take pity on us and help us." "If you can?" said Jesus. "Everything is possible for one who believes." Immediately the boy's father exclaimed, "I do believe; help me overcome my unbelief!"* —Mark 9:22-24

What I see in these verses is a father who was struggling to navigate the emotional turmoil and confusion of watching his child suffer. I know that feeling well. I can relate to the father in this story. Many times, through our thirty-year season of storms, I have found myself in intense battles with discouragement and confusion due to the repeated attacks on my family's health. Nothing in my life experience has caused me to feel more helpless than watching my children suffer with life-threatening health issues. Through decades of ministry, I have walked with countless families through tragic situations. One of the most difficult aspects of those times of crisis was having to watch a beloved family member suffer.

> ## Struggles with uncertainty can be caused by watching a loved one suffer.

Living Under Constant Attack

One of the most obvious portrayals in the Old Testament of a person who experienced times of uncertainty is King David. Many times, he began a psalm with a question or complaint and ultimately ended the psalm with praise. Clearly, David experienced times of God's miraculous favor as well as times of devastating disaster. Psalm 3 perfectly illustrates the main theme of this chapter. It was written during the period when David was fleeing from his son Absalom who was attempting to steal the kingdom:

"Lord, how many are my foes! How many rise up against me! Many are saying of me, 'God will not deliver him. But you are a shield around me, O Lord, you bestow glory on me and lift up my head. To the Lord I cry aloud, and he answers from his holy hill." —Psalm 3:1-4

Psalm 3 aligns with a pattern that we often see in David's writings. He begins this psalm by acknowledging the chaos of his reality and then shifts his focus to his confidence in God. There is a valuable lesson in this for us. It is healthy to acknowledge our feelings, but we can't allow them to control us. Emotions are real, but they don't always represent reality. Acknowledging our feelings and then focusing on our faith is a helpful strategy in times of trouble.

> ## Emotions are real, but they don't always represent reality.

It would be difficult to imagine the level of personal betrayal that David felt when he realized that his own son was attempting to steal the kingdom. Have you ever been betrayed by someone that you loved and trusted? Your answer to that question is almost certainly yes.

Perhaps you had a close friend with whom you shared some very private details about issues you were dealing with, only to find out later that your trusted friend betrayed your confidence and spread gossip about your situation all over town. Possibly you have experienced betrayal or attacks from some of your coworkers who were attempting to make themselves look better by making you look bad in front of your boss. Or maybe you have been betrayed by an unfaithful spouse who broke their vows and broke your heart.

Attacks can come in many different forms. One of the most unusual examples of this is one of my friends—Zach—who served in the military and was deployed in Afghanistan in an active war zone. His unit came under attack many times, but he survived and made it back home. After his return to the United States, he began to experience a variety of physical health issues that were likely related to his time in the Middle East.

The most unusual example of attacks on his health was due to severe allergic reactions that he experienced as a result of bee or wasp stings. Over a period of about ten years, Zach was rushed to the hospital over thirty-eight times after suffering major health incidents that required him to be put on a breathing machine due to anaphylactic shock from these stings. He also experienced approximately one hundred minor incidents that required medical intervention without a breathing machine. I had never heard of anyone getting stung so often. As a result of all the bee and wasp stings, doctors performed dozens of tests and suspected that Zach's body was producing pheromones that literally attracted bees and wasps to him to the extent that he could not even walk outside without getting stung.

Further investigation revealed that this situation was likely caused by his exposure to certain chemicals during his time in the Middle East. It is incredibly ironic that Zach made it through several years of deployment in an active war zone and survived exposure to all those bullets—and yet his life has been threatened repeatedly because of exposure to bees. Have you ever struggled to understand a season of repeated attacks?

> Struggles with uncertainty can be caused by feeling like you're living under constant attack.

Feeling Overwhelmed

In this last few pages, we have seen portrayals of a struggling prophet, a struggling parent, a struggling psalmist, and several other struggling people. Of all the examples in this chapter of people who struggled with uncertainty, this next one is, without a doubt, the most unexpected and the most illuminating. We have all struggled with uncertainty at some point, and it is not surprising to hear of others around us or even biblical characters who have wrestled with it as well. But we have much to glean from this next example:

Then Jesus went with his disciples to a place called Gethsemane, and he said to them, "Sit here while I go over there and pray." He took Peter and the two sons of Zebedee along with him, and he began to be sorrowful and troubled. Then he said to them, "My soul is overwhelmed with sorrow to the point of death. Stay here and watch with me."

Going a little farther, he fell with his face to the ground and prayed, "My Father, if it is possible, may this cup be taken from me. Yet not as I will, but as you will." —Matthew 26:36-39

POWERFUL STRATEGIES TO DEAL WITH UNCERTAINTY

This scene in the garden took place on the night that Jesus was arrested before being crucified the next day. Obviously, it was a high-stress moment for the Lord. There are several principles in these verses that are relevant to us when a storm is coming. As always, Jesus is the ultimate example for us to follow. As we look more closely at the scene in the garden that night, our Lord's actions convey valuable strategies that can help us deal with seasons of uncertainty.

The first thing we see is that *Jesus did not isolate Himself* during this time of intense pressure. He took His disciples with Him to the garden to pray. Many times, we tend to withdraw from others when we are facing a stressful time of uncertainty. That response is often motivated by pride because we don't want others to know that we are struggling.

Isolation is a common tactic that Satan tries to use against us because he knows that he has a better chance of taking us out if we are not surrounded by our brothers and sisters in Christ. I have seen this same principle played out during a safari on the Serengeti in Africa. The tour guide parked our vehicle on a small hill as we were watching a lion sneaking up on a herd of gazelles. As the gazelles were grazing, there was one that fell behind and was separated from the herd. When the lion launched his attack, he didn't run into the middle of the herd—he targeted the gazelle that was isolated. Don't be that gazelle!

Second, *Jesus had an inner circle* comprised of the three disciples that He was closest to—Peter, James, and John. He invited all the disciples to pray with Him in the garden, but He took His closest friends aside and shared more details with them than He did with the others. Many of us have learned in life that *you can't tell everything to everyone.* When your private prayer request is shared on social media by someone you thought you could trust, that is a sign that you need to tighten up your inner circle. We all need a small group of trusted friends that has proven its loyalty over time. We are not designed to walk through life alone.

Third, *Jesus shared the most intimate details of His thoughts and feelings with His inner circle.* One benefit of cultivating that small group of trusted friends is that we don't have to filter our thoughts and feelings with them. We all need that tight group with whom we can be completely transparent. I've often wondered what it was like for those closest to Jesus to see the Lord in such visible distress and hear Him say, "My soul is overwhelmed with sorrow to the point of death." To hear these words spoken by the Son of God, whom they had seen heal the sick, raise the dead, cast out demons, multiply the fish and loaves, and walk on water—must have been shocking. But it should be encouraging to us to realize that even Christ Himself faced struggles of this sort. Don't keep your emotions bottled up inside. Open up to those who have proven themselves trustworthy.

Fourth, Jesus didn't stop with just bearing His soul to His friends. *He went further, fell to the ground and prayed to His heavenly Father.* As helpful as it is to have our friends and our trusted inner circle—they can't take the place of our time alone with God. To navigate uncertainty, we can't just vent to our friends; we must go farther and pour our heart out to God. And we also need to stay in His presence long enough to hear His response. Jesus prayed, "My Father, if it is possible, may this cup be taken from me."

Obviously, Jesus was not looking forward to the intense physical suffering He was about to endure. But I don't think He was just referring to the physical pain. The cup that Jesus was speaking of was the cup of God's wrath that would be poured out on Him as He took on Himself the sins of all humanity throughout the ages: "God made him who had no sin to be sin for us, so that in him we might become the righteousness of God," (2 Corinthians 5:21). Clearly, He was uncertain if that aspect of the Father's plan was nonnegotiable because He asked if the cup could be taken from him.

Fifth, after Jesus poured His heart out to our heavenly Father, *He concluded His prayer with these words, "Yet not as I will, but as you will."* This is another powerful lesson for us. It is totally appropriate for us to acknowledge our feelings, vent to our friends, and pour out our hearts to God in prayer when we are under great stress and wrestling with uncertainty. But after all those things are said and done, we need to place our trust in God and declare our submission to His plan— even when we don't understand it. In Jesus' prayer, He expressed *uncertainty* about whether He was required to endure the "cup" that was about to be poured out on him. But He also expressed *certainty* in His commitment to submit to God's will no matter what. We need to adopt this same mindset. As we follow the example of Christ in the toughest days of our lives, we need to allow the certainty of our commitment to obey God's will to override any uncertainty regarding the details of God's plan.

> As we follow the example of Christ in the toughest days of our lives, we need to allow the certainty of our commitment to obey God's will to override any uncertainty regarding the details of God's plan.

Some of the most practical truth in this chapter speaks to the issue of transparency which flows from a posture of humility. It demonstrates that we care more about the Lord's opinion than we do about what others think. The opposite response would be to hide our struggle and simply pretend that all is well. There are problems with that approach. First, if we are unwilling to admit that we are struggling, we are unlikely to receive the help we need. Second, the main motive for hiding our struggles is to maintain the appearance that everything is fine—when we know that it is not. That demonstrates that we value people's opinions above God's, and that flows from a posture of pride.

God's Word always encourages humility and discourages pride. Faith is the foundation of our relationship with God. Part of our problem is that we can tend to view a struggle with uncertainty as a sign of weak faith. But when you consider the list of people in this chapter who had issues with uncertainty, there is no way we could label any of those people as having weak faith!

It is important for us to remember that the Bible teaches that faith is a gift from God: "For it is by grace you have been saved, through faith—and this is not from yourselves, it is the gift of God" (Ephesians 2:8-9). The biblical view of faith frees us from the human constraints of having to act like we have it all together when we know inside that we don't. Faith is a gift from God that we receive humbly—not a badge of spirituality that we wear proudly. I chose the title *The Certainty of Uncertainty* for this chapter because anyone who is honest will admit that they have wrestled with doubts and uncertainty at some point.

> ## Faith is a gift from God that we receive humbly—not a badge of spirituality that we wear proudly.

A word of caution—faith environments that immediately and aggressively condemn the slightest hint of a struggle with uncertainty can become toxic and actually hinder our growth in God. That type of environment breeds pretense motivated by pride instead of honesty motivated by humility. We should always adopt a posture of humility in our walk with the Lord and keep in mind that our perception may not always be correct. We are all prone to blind spots, and that is one reason we need close, healthy relationships with trusted friends who are walking the pathway of faith beside us.

Practical Strategies to Overcome Doubt and Uncertainty

1) Embrace the truth that it's okay to be honest about your struggles. (Mark 9:23-24)

2) If Peter, David, John the Baptist and Jesus experienced uncertainty, you will too!

3) Don't isolate yourself from relationships—stay connected. (Matthew 26:36)

4) Maintain a trusted inner circle with whom you can be transparent. (Matthew 26:37)

5) Acknowledge your emotions, but don't let them control you. (Matthew 26:38)

6) Regularly pray and seek God. (Matthew 26:39, 42, 44)

7) Stay faithful and submit to God's will—no matter what. (Matthew 26:39)

REFLECTION & APPLICATION

1) Describe a time in your life when you battled with uncertainty.

2) Describe a time when you have overcome doubt and uncertainty.

3) Name three people in your life that you consider to be part of your inner circle.

4) If you don't have people who are currently close enough to be in your inner circle, who is in your life with whom you would choose to cultivate those close relationships? Whom do you trust the most?

SAMPLE PRAYER

Lord, I thank You for Your compassion and understanding of my struggles with uncertainty. I don't want to struggle with doubts, but sometimes, I do when the storms of life come. And when those battles erupt, I ask for Your Holy Spirit to comfort me, strengthen me, and lead me on the pathway of Your will to the other side of the storm. Help me to embrace the principles of Your Word and act on them regardless of what I'm facing. Help me to stay close to You and to my fellow believers as I avoid isolation in times of trouble. Give me the wisdom to choose a healthy inner circle and the humility to be honest about my struggles. I pray all of this in Jesus' name.

FAITH DECLARATION

Lord, I declare by faith that I will win every battle with doubt and uncertainty through the power of Your Word and the Holy Spirit. I declare that I will not isolate myself from You or from my fellow believers at times when I am struggling. Lord, I choose to consistently cultivate a close, healthy relationship with You and with my brothers and sisters in Christ. I will cast all my anxiety on You because You care for me. And I will choose to submit to Your divine plan for my life, even at times when my circumstances are confusing. When I don't understand—I will still stand! I declare all these things by faith in the name of Jesus!

CHAPTER 9

THE FOCUS OF FAITH

"'Lord, if it's you,' Peter replied, 'tell me to come to you on the water.'"
—Matthew 14:28

N ow we are approaching one of the most dramatic scenes in this story and one of the most astounding events in the entire Bible. Peter may have been impetuous, but I believe that he truly wanted to *follow* Jesus even if the pathway seemed impossible. Can you imagine the conversation that may have taken place when the other disciples realized that Peter was seriously considering climbing out of the boat to try to walk on the water like Jesus? "Are you crazy!? You can't walk on water! Just shut up and stay here in the boat with the rest of us."

> Anyone who raises their head above the crowd should be ready to dodge a few rocks because they will be thrown.

Of course, whatever conversations that may or may not have taken place were not recorded, so we can't know for sure what was said. But human nature is a pretty consistent indicator of such things. And we all have seen examples of what can happen when someone attempts something out of the ordinary. People who attempt great things often draw the ire of those who do not wish to be shown that there is more to life than just the status quo. Anyone who raises their head above the crowd should be ready to dodge a few rocks because they will be thrown.

Jesus answered Peter's request with a single word. "Come." With that one word, Peter got down out of the boat and took his first step on the surface of the water! When he stepped out of the boat, he was stepping out on faith. One day when I was studying this passage, a thought occurred to me. *It wasn't the water that was holding Peter up—it was the word from the Lord.* I believe that if Peter had attempted this feat without a word from the Lord, he would have lived up to his name and sunk like a rock. But because Peter received the word from the Lord to proceed, he was able to do the impossible. He was not only walking on the water, but he was also walking on the Word. Because Jesus had given him express permission to step out of the boat, the liquid elements complied with the command of their creator and buoyed Peter on top of the waves.

As I mentioned previously, one of the things that my family has learned through all of the storms we have experienced is that in order to survive the storm—you need a word from the Lord! During the darkest days of our most intense storms, we surrounded ourselves with the Word of God. In our times of crying out to the Lord and praying for His help, He led us to specific scriptures that encouraged our spirits and empowered our faith to trust Him for miraculous intervention on our behalf. And God did not disappoint.

Time after time, He showed up in our situation, and we would experience a sudden shift from things going all wrong to things improving rapidly. One of the most memorable examples of this kind of sudden turn came during Anna Grace's twelve-hour emergency brain surgery. After the surgery was finished and the surgeons came to give us the initial report, they were describing how difficult the process had been early on. They said that the tumor was extremely vascular and intertwined with the healthy tissue of Anna's brain.

They described a very arduous process in which it seemed as though they were not going to be able to remove all of the tumor. I believe the phrasing they used was something along the lines of, "This tumor was incredibly stubborn and just refused to cooperate." After hours of surgery, there began to be a sense that total resection was not going to be possible. And then, all of a sudden, everything changed. In their words, they said that it seemed as though after all those hours of tedious microsurgery, the tumor was suddenly loosened from the surrounding tissue, and they were able to remove it completely! There were thousands of people from all over the world praying for Anna Grace, and we were standing on the Word and believing for her healing. As was the case with all our storms, we needed a word to walk on. In the storms of your life, you will need a word from the Lord to carry you through.

Storms often catch us off guard, but they never surprise God. He is already present in our storm before we actually get there, and He has prepared the pathway to get us through it. Throughout the Word of God, we see a pattern. God doesn't just bring His people to the storm—He brings them through the storm! Since the Lord already knows the pathway through our times of adversity, it is imperative that we seek Him for His wisdom.

> Storms often catch us off guard, but they never surprise God. He is already present in our storm before we actually get there, and He has prepared the pathway to get us through it.

As we have already discussed in a previous chapter, every storm we will ever face is under His feet. He is the master over the things that frighten us, and He has a word for us to walk on that will get us through to the other side. The reason that Peter was successful in doing the impossible was because he was acting in obedience to the word of the Lord. So, we need to embrace the fact that obedience to the word of the Lord also puts the storm under *our* feet!

This is a principle that is confirmed in other scriptures as well:

Everyone has heard about your obedience, so I am full of joy over you, but I want you to be wise about what is good, and innocent about what is evil. The God of peace will soon crush Satan under your feet. —Romans 16:19-20

Did you get that? God will not only defeat Satan by crushing him under the feet of Christ, but this verse indicates that God will crush Satan under our feet when we are consistently walking the pathway of faith in obedience to God's will and in alignment with His destiny for our lives. No one else in the boat had the courage or faith to even ask permission to make an attempt. The Bible records that Peter got down out of the boat, walked on the water, and came toward Jesus. Obeying the Lord's instructions empowered him to do something he could never do on his own.

THE MIRACLE IS IN THE COMMAND

When we examine this event, something becomes clear. The miracle was in the command. When Jesus spoke the instruction for Peter to come to Him walking on water, He was authorizing the miracle to take place. The only variable that remained was whether or not Peter would act on the word of Jesus. When Peter's faith flowed out into obedience, the miracle was assured. This principle is displayed throughout the Scriptures. The miracle is in the command—if we obey the command, then we can access the miracle.

There are numerous examples of this principle in the Bible. In Joshua 3, Joshua was preparing to lead the people of Israel across the Jordan River. The scripture indicated that the Jordan was at flood stage during those days, so there was likely a lot of concern on the part of the people. God gave Joshua some specific instructions. He gave him a word to walk on. When Joshua obeyed the word and instructed the priests to follow it, the miracle took place. As soon as the feet of the priests who carried the ark touched the river's edge, God caused the waters upstream to be cut off and stop flowing! The priests who carried the ark of God stood firm in the middle of the Jordan—on dry ground! After that, all the people crossed over on dry ground. They obeyed the command, and they accessed the miracle.

In Luke 17, we find the account where Jesus healed ten men who had leprosy. While they were still afflicted, Jesus instructed them to go show themselves to the priest to verify that they were cleansed. The Bible says that as they went, they were healed. They obeyed the command, and they accessed the miracle! In each of these cases and numerous others, we see a pattern of people stepping out in faith to obey the Lord, and suddenly, they accessed the miracle that they desperately needed.

STUMBLING IN FEAR

"But when he saw the wind, he was afraid and, beginning to sink, cried out, 'Lord, save me!'" The first word of this verse reveals one of the annoying aspects of life. It seems that there is always a "but." As much as we would love to just live a life of smooth sailing, we have already seen that generally does not work out. There always seems to be some challenge, some problem, or some crisis that interrupts our flow and distracts our focus. As we read these verses from the safety and security of our comfy chair, we can tend to be a little tough on Peter. We think thoughts like, *Why in the world did you take your eyes off Jesus? You had it made! You were walking on the water! All you had to do was stay focused on the Lord, but you blew it!*

While there may indeed be some merit in these thoughts, before we throw too many stones at Peter, maybe we should take inventory of our own life. How many times have we taken our eyes off the Lord and started to sink? How many times have we gotten distracted by life's stormy winds and crashing waves that were tossing us all over the place? The truth is that all of us have been guilty of the same pattern of weakness that we judge in Peter's life as he started to slip into the depths. As long as Peter was focused on Jesus, he was walking in faith on the word he had received. But when he got distracted by the wind and waves, his focus shifted to the threats that surrounded him. What are you looking at? What are you focused on? Focus is huge! Our focus either empowers our faith or empowers our fear!

> ## Our focus either empowers our faith or empowers our fear!

If we focus on the Lord and His Word, our faith is empowered. If we focus on the crisis around us, our fear is empowered. Peter's focus led to his fear.

In my personal life, as well as in over thirty-five years of gospel ministry, it has become evident to me that the go-to strategy that the enemy uses to paralyze God's people is fear! He consistently uses fear as a weapon to keep people discouraged and distracted from their destiny. The Greek word that translates as "afraid" in this text is the word *phobeo*. Does that word look vaguely familiar? It kind of reminds you of our English word "phobia." There's a good reason for that. *Phobeo* in this verse literally means to "run away in terror." A phobia, according to *Merriam-Webster*, is "an exaggerated usually inexplicable and illogical fear of a particular object, class of objects, or situation."[3]

When Peter's focus shifted off of Jesus and onto the stormy winds and waves, he was suddenly gripped with an extreme terror—the kind of fear that provokes us to run away from our situation and try to find a safe place. On the surface, I don't necessarily think of Peter's fear as being irrational. After all, he was outside the boat, literally walking among the crashing waves. It's difficult to conceive of that being a peaceful stroll.

But when we look closer and analyze the situation, our perception changes. Yes, Peter was outside the safety of the boat. Yes, he was

---

3 "Phobia," *Merriam-Webster.com Dictionary*, https://www.merriam-webster.com/dictionary/phobia.

exposed to the furious elements that surrounded him. Yes, he was literally doing the impossible (which can always be scary). But when you really think about it, Peter was in the safest place that he could possibly be—walking obediently in the very center of God's will.

Not only that, but like so many other places in Scripture where God's people were facing down a potentially dangerous storm, he was not alone. Jesus was right there in front of him, encouraging him to keep moving forward—to keep walking closer to Jesus. When you think of it that way, Peter didn't realize it, but there was actually no safer place in the world for him to be in that moment than right there in the middle of that storm. Why?

Because that's where Jesus was. Jesus was not only mastering that storm's wind and waves, He was also empowering Peter to do exactly the same thing. And when Peter's focus shifted and his fear took hold, his instinctive reaction is described by a word that means to "flee in terror." Herein lies the problem; when you flee in fear from the center of God's will, you always end up in a more dangerous place. Peter's desire was to get to a place of safety, but his fear led him in exactly the opposite direction. He left the safety of the water's surface and began to slip down into the depths.

How many times have we allowed fear to take over and cause us to run away from the Lord instead of continuing to walk towards him? I can confirm that in my own life, I have put myself in far greater peril while running away from God than I ever have while moving towards him. As so often happens in our human nature, Peter's instincts betrayed him. What he desired was greater safety; what he got was greater danger.

If you find yourself in the middle of a storm that the Lord has purposely sent you into, you need to realize that because He is there with you, that is actually the safest place for you to be. It won't feel like it, and your human nature will want nothing more than to escape.

Be very careful because if you choose to retreat from God's will, you will only end up in a worse situation. There will be times in your life when the enemy of your soul will use *scare tactics* to discourage you from following the path of your destiny in God's kingdom. Don't allow that to happen.

REFLECTION & APPLICATION

1) Describe a time when your focus empowered your faith.

2) Describe a time when your focus empowered your fear.

3) Is there a word from the Lord that fear has hindered you from stepping out on? What do you believe the Lord is saying to you about this?

SAMPLE PRAYER

Lord, I pray that You will help me to keep my focus on You in the good times and in the bad times. Please speak Your word into my life and give me the faith to step out of my comfort zone and into the pathway of my God-given destiny. I bind Satan's attempts to distract my attention away from You, Lord, by drawing my focus to the problems around me. I pray that as I walk in obedience to

Your Word, You will crush the works of Satan under my feet. I pray these things in the mighty name of Jesus! Amen!

FAITH DECLARATION

Lord, I declare by faith that I will keep my focus on You by spending time in prayer, worship, and the Word. As You speak divine direction into my life, I will step out in obedience to walk in faith and follow You. When the storms arise, I will not be distracted by the swirling circumstances, but I will keep my eyes on You. I declare these things by faith in the name of Jesus!

CHAPTER 10

RESCUE, RESTORATION, AND REFLECTION

*"But when he saw the wind, he was afraid and, beginning
to sink, Peter cried out, 'Lord, save me!' And immediately,
Jesus reached out his hand and caught him...."*
—Matthew 14:30-31

DISTRACTION OR TRACTION?

As we have already discussed, the shifting of Peter's focus from the Lord to the storm was the reason he lost his footing on the water's surface and began to sink. As I was reading these verses years ago, the Lord dropped a thought into my spirit that has helped me greatly in times of trouble. Because Peter stepped out in faith in obedience to the word of the Lord, he was given supernatural *traction* to walk on the water. But when he shifted his focus off the Lord and onto his circumstances, that *distraction caused him to lose his traction* and begin to sink.

The prefix –dis is used in many cases to portray the opposite of whatever word it is combined with. For example, disbelief is the opposite of belief, and disappear is the opposite of appear. I believe that *distraction* is the opposite of *traction*. This is the reason that the enemy of our soul constantly tries to keep us focused on our problems. The devil knows that if he can flood our lives with distraction, he can cause us to lose our traction. The greatest threat to the kingdom of darkness is when we, as believers, keep our focus on Christ and gain traction on the pathway to our divine destiny. At Peter's moment of crisis, his focus shifted back to the Lord, and he cried out for help. So often, this is the case for all of us. We lose our focus on the Lord and start to fall. Then, when we realize that we are in trouble, we call out to Him for help.

> The devil knows that if he can flood our lives with distraction, he can cause us to lose our traction.

There are some other things about this verse that I have always loved. The scripture says that when Peter cried out to the Lord, Jesus *immediately reached out* His hand and rescued Peter. This verse is a testament to the love and compassion of our Lord. In our human nature, we tend to react to failure in the lives of others with a judgmental attitude. We think, and sometimes, say things like "Well, that's what you get for taking your eyes off the Lord. You should have known better. What did you think was going to happen?" But that is not how

Jesus responded to failure. He *immediately* came to Peter's rescue and pulled him up from the water. That's what the Lord does—He pulls us up out of the messes we have made. In your worst storms and your most embarrassing moments when you cry out to the Lord, He will reach out to you!

> In your worst storms and your most embarrassing moments when you cry out to the Lord, He will reach out to you!

The Lord does not delight in our failure, but He does delight in pulling us up out of it.

One day as I was reading these verses, another thought occurred to me. If Jesus was able to *immediately* reach out to take hold of Peter, that means that when Peter began to sink, he had almost made it to Jesus. That realization sparked a question in my mind. *How many times do we get distracted and lose focus when our goal is literally within our reach?* I have seen a pattern in life and in ministry that convinces me that storms tend to intensify when we are closer to victory than we realize. I believe it is a major tactic of the enemy to try to distract us from the path towards Jesus in order to keep us from walking in our God-given destiny.

WHY DID YOU DOUBT?

Jesus' first words to Peter after stopping his descent were, "You of little faith, why did you doubt?" These words are always taken as a reprimand, and they may very well be, but I do not believe that Jesus spoke these words in a harsh tone. When I read them, in my mind's eye, Jesus is speaking them with a grin. Later, He went on to teach His disciples that it is not necessary to have *huge faith*. Specifically, He said that if they possessed faith the size of a mustard seed, nothing would be impossible for them. So, when I read Jesus' words, I don't register a harsh rebuke but possibly more of a good-natured *jab* at Peter for losing his focus and snatching defeat from the jaws of victory.

So, what was the purpose of the question? Jesus already knew what led to Peter's lapse. He was not asking the question so that He could get clarity *from* Peter. He was asking the question so that Peter could understand what caused him to lose his focus on Jesus. It seems odd that he would give in to doubt after he was already walking on the surface of the water. He was already breaking the laws of physics. He was in the process of doing the impossible when he started to doubt that doing the impossible was indeed possible.

No one ever said that our human nature is logical. The truth is that we often struggle with doubt long after we have piled up more than sufficient evidence that our faith was well-founded. This can tend to happen when we ask the wrong questions. I have struggled with doubt in various capacities throughout my life. I have found that my struggle with doubt is intensified when I begin to dwell on one question: why? Why did God allow so much suffering in my family? Why have my kids had to repeatedly face life-or-death battles beginning in their infancies? Why?

The problem with dwelling on the question, "Why?" is that we do not yet see the end of the story. Sometimes a movie doesn't make sense until the end. At times, I have allowed myself to get stuck in my unanswered questions, and that is not a healthy place to be. If I am honest with myself, when I ask God why, that question usually results from an attack on my comfort. I have learned (repeatedly) that to move forward, I have to put aside the incessant drive to understand the *why* and shift my focus to better questions.

Rather than asking why, I need to ask *what* and *how*. Lord, *what* are you wanting to teach me through this situation? What are you saying to me? Also, I need to ask how. How do you want me to respond to this situation? How can I cooperate with your plan to play my role in this circumstance correctly? As I stated earlier, we sometimes struggle with doubt long after we have more than sufficient evidence to believe.

> Rather than asking why, I need to ask what and how. Lord, what are you wanting to teach me through this situation? How do you want me to respond to this situation? How can I cooperate with your plan to play my role in this circumstance correctly?

In recent years, if I allowed myself to once again begin to question the why, I would eventually begin to look at all the miraculous things that God has done in our lives. Even though I still don't understand everything we have faced, I cannot ignore the big picture. We are all extremely blessed just to be alive! I choose to celebrate the fact that we are all still here even though the odds were against us. It doesn't make sense to begin to doubt when you are already walking on the water. But that's what Peter did, and that's what we often do. To recap,

I believe that Jesus' purpose in asking the question was to help Peter identify where he went wrong and learn from his mistake. Jesus was lifting Peter up spiritually as He was lifting him up physically.

There is another detail that is often overlooked in this account. Verse 32 begins with, "And when they had climbed back into the boat...." Did you see that? *They* climbed back into the boat. How did they get back to the boat? *They* walked on the water to get back. With all the focus on Peter's struggle with doubt and fear, people tend to totally miss that fact: AFTER Peter lost his focus (and his buoyancy), Jesus lifted him back up on top of the water, and Peter miraculously walked on the water with Jesus the entire distance back to the boat! It would seem to me that Peter's lapse of faith is the most insignificant part of this story when you really examine it. He spent far more time walking on the water than he did sinking. This record-breaking stroll was certainly not flawless, but it was far more of a success than a failure.

Some people might question my characterization of Peter's *short stroll on the sea* as successful. I know that I have often heard the whole ordeal portrayed as a failure because Peter took his eyes off the Lord and began to sink. But I would assert a different perspective. Other than Jesus, human history has only ever recorded one person who walked on the surface of the sea—and that one person was Peter. Without question, his walk was abbreviated by his battle with fear and distraction, but in the arena of *water-walking* he still placed second in the world. And a silver medal is nothing to be ashamed of!

REFLECTION

Very few experiences in life are 100 percent positive or 100 percent negative—100 percent successful or 100 percent failure. Most things are a mixture of positive and negative, and they generally fall somewhere on a spectrum between the two. But even in situations when the upside far outweighs the downside, we tend to focus on the negative, even when it is tiny by comparison. In this way, we cheat ourselves not only out of a legitimate victory celebration but also the accompanying gratitude for the blessing of the Lord.

Countless times in my decades of ministry, I have seen people who have a legitimate reason to celebrate God's blessing and favor in their lives. Instead, they choose to focus on one negative element to the point that they lose all sense of perspective, and, like Peter, they begin to sink into the depths for no good reason. Speaking of sinking into the depths, this would be an appropriate juncture for us to consider another significant issue.

In an earlier chapter, we dealt with the principles of 2 Corinthians 10:4-5 and how they relate to our thought life. It is not just our thoughts, though, that can present a challenge. When our emotions kick in, we face an even greater struggle. Clearly, we are not emotionless Spock-like creatures who operate strictly in the realm of facts and logic. Our emotions can present a huge challenge when it comes to keeping our focus. In my struggles with unanswered questions, it was not just my thoughts that challenged me; it was how I felt about the situations.

Our emotions have the potential to drag us into the depths of depression and despair if we do not exercise our authority over them. As I was writing this chapter, the world was still in the throes of the COVID-19 pandemic. Life during those days was a perfect example of the impact and influence that our emotions can exert—often completely overriding our ability to think logically. Statistically, there has been a significant increase in the incidences of depression, anxiety, and other mental challenges since COVID-19 began. In many cases, people whose lives had not been drastically affected in a negative sense were struggling emotionally because everything in that season was so unfamiliar and foreign to our typical lifestyles.

There is an important principle here that is easy to miss: Feelings follow thoughts. This principle first became obvious to me many years ago when Nancy and I began to do a lot of marriage counseling with couples who were struggling. Over and over, we would see this principle demonstrated in the lives of couples whose marriages had become extremely unhealthy and dysfunctional. In the process of assessing a couple to determine their issues, we would often hear things like, "I still love him, but I'm not *in* love with him anymore." We would hear the same statement from husbands about their wives. Most of the time, those words would be communicated with a sense of grief because the person speaking them was convinced that once those *feelings* of being in love were gone, they would never return.

Then, time after time, with many different couples, we saw an amazing restoration of those long-lost feelings. How did it happen? Their feelings followed their thoughts. Think of a train on the railroad tracks. Most of the time, the engine is in the front, and it is pulling the railcars along behind it. Wherever the engine goes, the rest of the train has no choice but to follow (unless there's a train wreck). And we've seen a few of those in our counseling ministry as well.

Our thoughts are like an engine that pulls our emotions down the tracks. Where our thoughts go, our feelings follow. The reason that couples lost those loving feelings is because they stopped thinking loving thoughts. Their thoughts became saturated with criticism and complaints about what their spouse was doing wrong or not doing at all. We have actually worked with couples who could not seem to come up with a single positive comment about each other because their unbridled criticism had so tainted their perception that they couldn't even recognize each other's good qualities anymore.

> Our thoughts are like an engine that pulls our emotions down the tracks. Where our thoughts go, our feelings follow.

But we have also seen miraculous turnarounds in couples. These would typically occur as both spouses would take responsibility for their contributions to the "mess" and then commit to working on themselves instead of focusing on their spouse. When they would see each other working to make positive changes in their own attitude and behavior, all of a sudden, they would start thinking different kinds of thoughts. As things begin to turn around in a relationship, we have heard women say things like, "Wow, that was so sweet of him to cancel his golf game to stay home and help me clean up around the house." We have heard equally enthusiastic husbands report, "She hasn't kissed me like that in years!"

So many times, we have seen new life and fresh affection breathed into relationships because, as they worked on their attitudes and thoughts, their behavior began to change. When they witnessed the change in behavior, they began to think positive thoughts about each other. When their thoughts focused on the positive, their emotions followed suit. And *viola*, amazing transformations took place.

The awareness of how our feelings follow our thoughts is not only relevant within the context of marriage relationships. It is a foundational principle of success in life. As we reflect on our life, we must be careful to maintain a balanced view of the whole picture. Even in the worst of times, there is something to celebrate. Forcing ourselves to acknowledge the positive can keep us from "sinking into the depths" of discouragement and depression just because we experienced a moment of failure.

INTERACTIVE ILLUSTRATION

Now is the perfect time to share a principle that changed my life. As I have shared it many times in presentations, I have had many people tell me that it changed their lives as well. This is not just a principle I want you to read—it is a truth with which I want you to actively engage. In order for you to experience this truth, you will need to follow these simple instructions:

1) Open the photos app on your cell phone.
2) Choose one of your favorite pictures.
3) Study the elements of what is in the picture, especially the corners and edges.
4) Zoom all the way in on that picture as far as you can.
5) Once again, take note of what you can see in the zoomed-in version of the picture.

Here is the takeaway: When you zoomed in on your photo, you could no longer see everything in the picture. You could only see the things that you had zoomed in on. That doesn't mean that the other elements of the photo were destroyed or deleted—it just means that you could no longer see the true reality of the whole picture because you had zoomed in on one aspect of it.

This is exactly what we do in times of trouble. Our focus is hijacked by the distraction of a crisis, and our perception zooms in so tightly on our trouble that we can no longer see the whole picture. All the things that were in the picture are still there—all the blessings and all of the things worth celebrating. But often, in times of a storm, we forget about the good things that are still a part of our lives because we have zoomed past them to focus on our adversity.

So, what's the solution? Zoom back out. Look at the big picture and let yourself experience the joy and gratitude that comes along with acknowledging the good things in life. This is a major reason that our family was able to *grow* through storms and not just *go* through storms! Early in our season of adversity, we cultivated a culture of celebration that reminded us to regularly zoom back out and pay attention to the blessings and not just the pain. We need to train ourselves to stare at the blessing and glance at the pain. In the account of Peter's stroll on the sea, we can choose to zoom in on his failure and let that element dominate our opinion, or we can look at the big picture and celebrate with him his silver medal in the sport of *water-walking*.

> We need to train ourselves to stare at the blessing and glance at the pain.

REFLECTION & APPLICATION

1) Recall a time when Satan flooded your life with distraction to cause you to lose traction on the pathway of God's will? Are you struggling with this right now?

2) If your focus is currently distracted from the pathway of God's will, what elements in this chapter can you engage to get you back on track?

3) In what ways has the enemy tempted you to zoom in on your problems and frustrations to the extent that you can no longer see the blessings of God that still inhabit your life? Decide today to zoom back out and see the big picture.

4) What areas of your life do you need to reevaluate based on the principles of this chapter? Have you skipped the celebration of victories and magnified the times of failure?

SAMPLE PRAYER

Lord, please forgive me for the times that I have shifted my focus from You to my problems. I thank You for all the times you have rescued me as I was sinking into the depths. When I am struggling to understand the circumstances of my life, please help me to ask better a question than why? Remind me to ask what You want me to learn, and how I can cooperate with Your plan. Please help me to monitor my thoughts and my emotions to keep them in alignment with Your will. I pray these things in Jesus' name!

FAITH DECLARATION

Lord, I declare by faith that I will do my best to keep my focus on You and not allow the devil to cause me to lose traction by attacking me with distraction. I declare that in times of failure, I will cry out immediately to You, and You will reach out immediately to me, just as You did for Peter. I choose to keep moving forward and never give up because when I feel like quitting, I could be one step away from victory, just like Peter. I declare that I will avoid the temptation to zoom in on my frustrations and keep my perspective on the full reality of the blessings of God in my life. I declare all these things by faith in the name of Jesus!

CHAPTER 11

WHEN THE WINDS DIE DOWN

"And when they had climbed back into the boat, the winds died down."
—Matthew 14:32

THE PURPOSE OF THE STORM

Was it a coincidence that the gale-force winds that had been battering the disciples all night long died down at the exact moment that Jesus and Peter climbed into the boat? I don't believe so. I think there is a significant lesson in the timing. What is the reason the winds ceased at that moment? They ceased when they were no longer needed. They had served their purpose. The Lord had a plan in mind from the moment He told the disciples to cross the lake. And His plan required high winds and rough seas.

> The Lord had a plan in mind from the moment He told the disciples to cross the lake. And His plan required high winds and rough seas.

When the storm winds are still blowing, it is difficult for us to see beyond the threats. Our survival mindset draws our attention to the wind and waves. Trying to identify God's purpose can be a challenge while the storm continues to rage. But when the winds die down, we seem to be able to see more clearly.

To help put this into context, we can recall a question that we alluded to earlier. "Lord, what are you wanting to teach me through this situation?" What do you think the Lord's agenda was for intentionally sending the disciples out into this storm? Clearly, Jesus wanted to strengthen their faith by demonstrating His authority over the laws of nature. The Lord was showing the disciples that the barriers that would hinder any ordinary man were no challenge to Him. The disciples would never have realized that Jesus could walk on water if they had not encountered the high winds and rough seas of this storm.

THE PATTERN: INSTRUCTION—OBSTRUCTION—CONSTRUCTION

If we take a step back from the details of this story and just look at the big picture, there are three phases that become obvious. Those phases are *instruction, obstruction,* and *construction.* These three elements align to a pattern that is not only seen often in the Scriptures but also in our lives. This whole event was launched when Jesus commanded the disciples to get into the boat and go ahead of Him to the other side of the lake. This instruction likely seemed inconsequential at the time. Since about seventy percent of the ministry of Christ took place near the northern shores of the Sea of Galilee, the disciples had crossed this lake many times.

But this time, after they obeyed the Lord's instruction—they faced a major obstruction. They probably thought that this would be a routine, uneventful sea crossing, but a storm developed that challenged their progress and tested their limits. Does this sound familiar? You obey an instruction from the Lord, and you expect smooth sailing. Then a storm blows up right in front of you. It not only hinders your path of obedience, but it also frightens you to the point that you question whether you will survive.

Any time we decide to obey the Lord, that decision will likely encounter an obstruction. You may have noticed that when you decide to make a positive change in your life, obstacles are virtually guaranteed. For instance, did you ever decide to start getting up an hour early every day to pray? What happened? The obstructions began to pile up. On the first day, you didn't want to get up because you had one of the best nights of sleep in your life. On the second day, you accidentally set your alarm for 5:30 p.m. instead of 5:30 a.m. On the third day, there was a power outage, and your alarm didn't go off. Obstruction is a predictable occurrence that often follows our obedience to the Lord.

> Following the instruction and overcoming the obstruction resulted in construction— the building up of their faith in Christ.

The next phase in the pattern is construction. Construction is the whole reason why the other phases take place. Jesus wanted to *construct* a whole new level of faith in His disciples, and that's exactly what happened. Their faith was built in an unprecedented way through this storm. Following the instruction and overcoming the obstruction resulted in construction—the building up of their faith in Christ.

At this point in their journey, the disciples had witnessed miraculous healings, demons cast out, the dead raised, and the feeding of the five thousand. As great as those miracles were, the gospel of Matthew does not record that the disciples declared Jesus to be the Son of God or that they worshiped Him after all the miracles that preceded this storm. The first time Matthew mentioned Jesus being worshiped by the disciples was immediately after He had walked on the stormy seas that threatened their lives and climbed into the boat as the winds died down:

> *And when they climbed into the boat, the wind died down. Then those who were in the boat worshiped him saying, "Truly, you are the Son of God."* —Matthew 14:32-33

We all enjoy the blessing that comes as the Lord multiplies His provision in our lives—but our faith leaps to another level when we witness His power over the storm that threatens us. When Jesus rescues us from death and destruction, we cannot help but declare His Lordship through worship!

Our family has experienced this many times through the years. As the Lord would bring us through a storm, our hearts would erupt in spontaneous celebration and worship of the One who had given us the victory. I can remember times when I victoriously raised my fists in the air after hearing a doctor's report that represented an incredible answer to prayer. Has the Lord ever built a deeper faith in your life by bringing you through a difficult storm? How did you feel when the winds died down, and you realized that God had rescued you? Was your heart filled with gratitude and praise for the God who walked on the troubled waters of your life and brought an end to the storm?

The Lord's plan obviously fulfilled His purpose in building the faith of the disciples to a whole new level. The men in that boat were the ones the Lord had chosen to spread the gospel after His resurrection. Their *resumes* might not have indicated that they were up to the task, yet they "turned the world upside down" (Acts 17:6, ESV) with the miraculous spread of the gospel. Even more impressive is the fact that it was done with no technology, no form of instant mass communication, and no way to accelerate the process. What they *did* have was the anointing of the Holy Spirit, the passion of an eyewitness to the resurrection, and the life lessons they had learned sitting at the feet of the greatest leader in history.

This pattern of instruction, obstruction, and construction is not only evident in the lives of the disciples of Christ. If we look closely, we can see this pattern in the lives of most biblical characters. God instructed Moses to go back to Egypt and bring the Israelites out of bondage. When Moses obeyed God and went back to Egypt, did he encounter any obstructions? Absolutely! God ended up unleashing a series of plagues to force Pharaoh to comply. Then, after victoriously leading the people out of Egypt, Moses and the Israelites faced another major obstruction—being trapped between the Egyptian army and the Red Sea. Then came the construction. God's people watched in awe as He demonstrated His ability to remove any obstruction or hindrance from their pathway forward. Can you imagine what it would have been like to watch the Lord open a dry passage through the Red Sea for you to escape from your enemies—and then to see them destroyed as they pursued you? The same waters that were held back in protection of Israel were released in judgment on their enemies.

This common pattern of instruction, obstruction, and construction also emerged as God sent Nehemiah to rebuild the broken walls of Jerusalem. After obeying the Lord's leading, Nehemiah went to Jerusalem to assess the situation. Guess what happened next? Nehemiah encountered multiple obstructions—lack of cooperation, ridicule from leaders, general threats of violence, and false accusations. During part of the rebuilding process, the workers had to do their work with swords strapped to their sides because of the threats of attack. But in spite of all the obstructions, the end result was construction. In this case, the construction was both physical and spiritual. The massive project of rebuilding the walls of Jerusalem was miraculously completed in fifty-two days. But it wasn't only the walls that were restored. Nehemiah 7 and 8 describe a renewal of worship in Jerusalem. The people's faith and commitment to worship God were rebuilt, and that *construction* was even more important than the city walls.

One of the most prominent examples of this pattern of instruction, obstruction, and construction can be seen in the life of the apostle Paul. Just a few days after his conversion to Christ, the Lord said of Saul, "This man is my chosen instrument to carry my name before the Gentiles and their kings and before the people of Israel" (Acts 9:15, BSB). God gave Saul a divine call and instruction like no other. The Lord's miraculous work in his life changed Saul into Paul and transformed him from a persecutor of the church into a preacher of the gospel.

Paul immediately began to proclaim the gospel of Christ. Within a few days of obeying God's instruction, Paul began to experience obstruction as he learned of a conspiracy to kill him. That's a huge storm to face as a new believer. But as we learned in an earlier chapter, intense heat and pressure over time not only transform cheap carbon into expensive diamonds—they also transform ordinary people into those whom God can use to accomplish extraordinary things. And the Lord revealed from the very beginning that Paul would experience unusual adversity: "I will show him how much he must suffer for my name" (Acts 9:16).

As time progressed, the pathway of God's will for Paul carried him through a stunning number of storms. Following are some verses from 2 Corinthians 11:23-28, that contain a *partial* listing of the obstructions that Paul faced as he followed the instructions of the Lord:

> *Are they servants of Christ? (I am out of my mind to talk like this.) I am more. I have worked much harder, been in prison more frequently, been flogged more severely, and been exposed to death again and again. Five times I received from the Jews the forty lashes minus one. Three times I was beaten with rods, once I was pelted with stones, three times I was shipwrecked, I spent a night and a day in the open sea, I have been constantly on the move. I have been in danger from rivers, in danger from bandits, in danger from my fellow Jews, in danger from Gentiles, in danger in the city, in danger in the country, in danger at sea, and in danger from false believers. I have labored and toiled and have often gone without sleep, I have known hunger and thirst and have often gone without food, I have been cold and naked. Besides everything else, I face daily the pressure of my concern for all the churches.*

Through the years, many have expressed shock at the amount of adversity our family has faced. But when I consider the hardships that the apostle Paul endured, it makes my troubles seem far less intense. The intensity of the obstruction that God allows often indicates the immensity of the construction that God intends. What God allowed

Paul to endure prepared him for the calling and impact that his life would make on the world.

> The intensity of the obstruction that God allows often indicates the immensity of the construction that God intends.

The obstructions that Paul encountered virtually disappear when compared to the construction that was accomplished through his life and ministry. Paul's accomplishments in gospel ministry are unmatched to this day. He made three long missionary journeys throughout the Roman empire. He established new churches, preached the gospel, and gave strength and encouragement to early Christians. Paul had a brilliant mind and an excellent grasp of philosophy and religion which enabled him to debate with the most educated scholars of the day. His clear explanations of the gospel in his letters to the early churches formed the foundation of Christian theology. Of the twenty-seven books of the New Testament, Paul is credited with having written thirteen of them.

Many of those epistles were written during some of Paul's most difficult days as he languished in prison for preaching the gospel. But God's plan for Paul from the beginning was *construction*. God used Paul to build people's faith in Christ on an unprecedented scale, and in this case, the construction did not cease when he breathed his last breath as a martyr for Christ at the hands of the Romans. The faith of virtually every follower of Christ has been impacted in a powerful way by the New Testament books that Paul wrote under the inspiration of the Holy Spirit. Our faith today is still being built through the ministry of a man who experienced an incomprehensible amount of adversity.

So, what should we do when the winds die down? Our first inclination is usually to celebrate the end of the storm. There is nothing wrong with that, but we need to do more. When the winds die down, and our fight or flight instincts fade, we can think more clearly and focus on the big picture. What is the Lord trying to teach me? What is He preparing me to do? What is my calling? When many people think of a "calling" from God, they envision the call to preach or pastor a church. Only a small fraction of believers are called to these assignments. But every follower of Christ is called to use their gifts and influence to spread the gospel and impact the lives of others.

The storm that the disciples feared would destroy them was actually being used by the Lord as *prep for their next step*. At that time, none of them understood the scope of God's plan to use them to change their world. So, when the winds die down, some good questions to ask might be, "Lord, what is my next step?" "What are You preparing me to do for Your kingdom?" "How can I grow from this experience?"

One of the greatest tragedies that can come from storms is enduring the obstruction but resisting the construction.

One of the greatest tragedies that can come from storms is when we endure the obstruction but resist the construction. Surviving a storm is a great blessing in that moment, but having our faith built up to a new level is an even greater blessing that never fades away.

One of the most inspiring characteristics in the life of Paul was that he didn't allow himself to be satisfied with what anyone else would consider unprecedented success. One of the verses in Paul's writings that indicate this truth is found in Philippians 3:12: "Not that I have already obtained all this, or have already arrived at my goal, but I press on to take hold of that for which Christ Jesus took hold of me." In spite of everything that Paul had accomplished for God, he possessed the humility to realize that he was not perfect, and he had not "arrived."

One of the most powerful elements of this verse is the phrase "I press on." This comes from the Greek word *dioko*. When used in a negative sense, this word was translated "to persecute." I think that is interesting given the fact that before he became a Christian, Paul was actively involved in persecuting the church. In a positive sense, *dioko* means to "earnestly pursue" or "to hunt or aggressively chase" like a hunter chasing his prey.

In my years of pastoring, I have had many church members and staff members who looked forward all year long to hunting season. They didn't just wander out into a field at random and bag their game. They planned their schedule differently during hunting season. They strategized, bought equipment, made preparations, and then sat up in a tree for hours in inclement weather just waiting for a deer to wander into range. Then, when the opportunity came, they took their shot.

I believe that Paul was inspired by the Holy Spirit to use this specific word to paint a picture of how committed he was to pursuing God's call. Even after so much success, he was totally focused on aggressively chasing the next step of God's plan for his life. This is a powerful example for us. Paul did not allow himself to get distracted by all the troubles he had faced. Instead, he chose to continue to focus on the next step that God was preparing for him.

For us to fulfill God's plan for our life, we must choose to focus on the purpose of the storm instead of the pain of the storm. In order to do that, we must choose to *press on* and continue to *hunt down* and *aggressively pursue* God's call on our life. When the winds die down after we've been through a storm, we need to make sure that our celebration is followed by evaluation. What is God saying? How is He building my faith? What next step is He leading me to take?

> For us to fulfill God's plan for our life, we must choose to focus on the purpose of the storm instead of the pain of the storm.

REFLECTION & APPLICATION:

1) Can you think of times in your life when the pattern of instruction, obstruction, and construction is now evident to you?

2) What was the instruction from the Lord that you followed?

3) What obstructions did you encounter?

4) How did God use adversity to construct a new level of faith in your life?

5) What do you believe God is calling you to do with your life?

6) In what ways are you aggressively pursuing God's direction?

7) What changes do you need to make in order to fully follow God's plan for your life?

SAMPLE PRAYER

Lord, I thank You for helping me to recognize that when the storm winds blow in my life, You always have a plan. And Your plan is not only to rescue me but also to refine me and raise me to a higher level of faith in Christ than ever before. Help me to remember that when the winds die down, it is fine for me to celebrate the calm, but I also need to investigate the call that You are developing in me. Lord, I don't believe that You are the cause of every storm, but I do believe that You will use every storm to propel me forward in faith. Help me to always keep my trust in You and my focus on Your pathway for my life. In Jesus' name, I pray! Amen.

FAITH DECLARATION

Lord, I declare by faith that just as the disciples worshiped You and rose to a new level of faith when their storm had passed, I, too, will worship You and allow You to build my faith to new levels with each storm that I face. I choose to obey Your instruction regardless of the obstruction in order to experience the construction of my faith to new levels. And like the apostle Paul, I choose to aggressively pursue every aspect of Your will for my life. I declare these things by faith in Jesus' name!

CHAPTER 12

PARTNERING WITH GOD

"When they had crossed over, they landed at Gennesaret.
And when the men of that place recognized Jesus, they sent
word to all the surrounding country. People brought all their
sick to him and begged him to let the sick just touch the edge
of his cloak, and all who touched him were healed."
—Matthew 14:34-36

A s we have previously stated, before their storm, the disciples saw
Jesus multiplying fish and loaves to feed the masses. But, on the
other side of their storm, they witnessed Christ totally transforming
people's lives by healing them of every sickness and disease. Knowing
that God has greater things in store for us on the other side of adversity should motivate us to partner with Him in every aspect of life.
This will require us to overcome some natural tendencies. When we
are engulfed in crisis, our human nature wants God to just snap His
fingers and magically make our troubles disappear. But God doesn't
do magic—he does miracles. And in virtually every miracle recorded

in the Bible, we find that God chooses to work through a partner who is willing to step out in faith and obey His instructions.

> When we are engulfed in crisis, our human nature wants God to just snap His fingers and magically make our troubles disappear.

Partnering with God brings many benefits into our lives. One of those benefits is access to *peace that passes all understanding*. This is a level of peace that doesn't seem to make sense in light of our circumstances. Through the years, in our darkest days, I have often had people ask me how our family was thriving in the midst of such adversity. My response to those questions always highlighted God's gracious gift of supernatural peace.

Acts 27 records a literal storm in the life of the apostle Paul. There are several elements in this story that can empower a supernatural peace in our lives in times of trouble. *First, God always has a plan.* We must never forget this important truth. As Paul and his shipmates were in the middle of a life-threatening storm, he displayed a calm confidence while everyone around him was in full panic mode. What made the difference? Why was Paul able to remain calm and experience supernatural peace while the ship was being battered by the storm?

The reason was that Paul had heard from God. And he relayed God's message to the others that were in the storm:

*Last night an angel of the God to whom I belong and whom
I serve stood beside me and said, "Do not be afraid, Paul. You
must stand trial before Caesar, and God has graciously given
you the lives of all who sail with you. So, keep up your courage,
men, for I have faith in God that it will happen just as he
told me. Nevertheless, we must run aground on some island."*
—Acts 27:23-25

As we covered in an earlier chapter, it is vital in times of adversity to seek the Lord for a word to help you navigate your situation. Receiving this word from God completely changed Paul's perception of his circumstances. We may not always understand when our pathway takes us into a storm—but it is a source of great comfort when we are reminded that God always has a plan.

Second, God always has a partner. As a servant of God, Paul had a part to play in God's plan. Part of Paul's responsibility was to share the word that God gave him with those around him in the storm. As he did that, there were specific instructions given to the crew that brought them into partnership with God's plan as well. We will cover those elements in the next chapter. This principle of partnership with God is obvious throughout the entire Bible. God has chosen to work *with* and *through* people who will put their trust in him.

Think of virtually any miracle in the Scriptures, and you will find God using someone to fulfill His agenda. God can obviously do whatever He wants to do. He does not *need* a partner to help him accomplish His plans—but evidence suggests that the Lord *prefers* to involve a person in the process. There are far more examples of this principle than we could ever cover in a single chapter or even in an entire book. So, we will focus on some of the most significant episodes where God selected a partner.

God recruited Moses to be His partner. Clearly, God demonstrated His awesome power as He unleashed plague after plague on the Egyptians to motivate them to set His people free. God could have broken the chains of bondage off the nation of Israel without Moses. But when we look at the significant events in the life of Moses, even from his birth, it is obvious that God was preparing Moses for a divine call to lead the nation of Israel. Having been born a Hebrew and raised in Pharoah's palace uniquely qualified Moses for the call of God on his life.

As the children of Israel departed Egypt on their way to the Promised Land, they soon found themselves in a crisis. Pursued by Pharaoh's army with their backs against the Red Sea, Israel questioned Moses and complained about their situation. But God had already plotted their miraculous pathway on dry ground through the midst of the Red Sea. God did not *need* Moses' help to split the sea and dry the ground, but He involved Moses anyway:

> *"Raise your staff and stretch out your hand over the sea to divide the water so that the Israelites can go through the sea on dry ground.*
>
> *Then Moses stretched out his hand over the sea, and all that night the Lord drove the sea back with a strong east wind and turned it into dry land. The waters were divided and the Israelites went through the sea on dry ground, with a wall of water on their left and on their right."* —Exodus 14:16, 21-22

Moses obeyed the Lord's instruction, and God performed the miracle.

God recruited David to be his partner. The giant known as Goliath was the most feared soldier on any battlefield in that era. God could have easily slain Goliath without involving a human being in the process. But, as is often the case, God chose the most unlikely candidate for the job—a teenage boy named David. Although David didn't have any military experience, he had proved himself faithful to the task of protecting his father's flock by engaging in battle with a lion and a bear. He was also faithful in a lifestyle of worshiping God from the depths of his soul.

As David stepped onto the battlefield and defended the name of his God against the enemies of Israel, I believe the Holy Spirit empowered David and even enhanced the skills he already possessed. No doubt David had developed considerable expertise in using a slingshot to defend the sheep, but with the battle armor that Goliath was wearing, there were very few places on his body that were vulnerable to attack. One of those places was the opening around his eyes in the bronze battle helmet he was wearing. And that was exactly where the rock from David's sling landed! Yes, I believe that David was skilled with a sling, but I also believe that God supernaturally directed that rock to the one place that would defeat the giant. These examples confirm a pattern seen throughout the Scriptures. God employs an obedient person of faith to play a part in His divine agenda. These divine partnerships did not end with the biblical narrative.

God is recruiting YOU to be His partner! Just like Moses and David, you were born with a divine destiny to fulfill. But, as we have seen, God has chosen to accomplish His purposes through people who love Him and are faithful to His call. The examples of Moses and David line up with every other biblical character. God uses those who submit to His will and obey His Word. God will use your life in greater ways than you could ever imagine—IF you are willing to submit to His will and obey His Word.

> God will use your life in greater ways than you could ever imagine—IF you are willing to submit to His will and obey His Word.

This brings us to another important aspect of partnering with God. Romans 8:14 declares a key principle that we must embrace: "For as many as are led by the Spirit of God, they are the sons of God." The word translated as "led" in this verse comes from the Greek word *agontai*. This word was often used to picture leading an animal with a rope tied around its neck. Those of us who are dog lovers are very familiar with this image. Walking a dog with a leash aligns pretty well with the image created by this Greek word, although in those days, it probably referred to using a rope to lead a cow or a goat.

Why would the Lord choose this word to help us understand the principles of being led by the Holy Spirit? I believe the reason is because a cooperative animal can easily be led with a *gentle tug* on the rope—but a stubborn animal requires much more pressure from the rope to *drag* it in the right direction. Partnership with God is actually easier when we cultivate and maintain a sensitivity to the Holy Spirit as He *tugs* at our heart to lead us in the path of God's will.

As we follow the Lord's leading, He will not only use us to bless others, but He will also bless our lives with abundant favor as we partner with Him. Have you ever experienced a time in your life when you genuinely needed a miracle from God? Obviously, I have been there many times, and each time, I had a part to play in God's plan. If you need a miracle in your finances, you can't just blow all your cash on stuff that doesn't matter. You must *order* your finances with wisdom according to God's Word, be disciplined in your stewardship, and trust God to do His part.

If we want God's blessing on our physical health, we should partner with Him by living a healthy lifestyle, taking care of the body He has given us, and trusting Him to do His part. If you are married and want your marriage to be happy and healthy, you can't just ignore the biblical principles of marriage and live according to your feelings and emotions. Healthy, happy marriages are consistently cultivated by people who are committed to building their relationship on the principles of God's Word. If you choose to consistently partner with God, you will be amazed at the blessing and favor that will flow—not only *in* your life but also *through* your life as God uses you to impact others.

Finally, God always has a purpose. This is a truth that we have illustrated in many chapters of this book. The angel confirmed to Paul that God's plan was for him to testify before Caesar. That knowledge, along with God's promise to protect the lives of all the others on board the ship, strengthened Paul's confidence that he would make it through the storm. But at the time, Paul did not realize that God also had plans to use him to bring the gospel to people on the island of Malta as well as to the Jewish people living in Rome. For two years in Rome, Paul was allowed to stay in his own rented house and share the gospel with everyone he encountered.

As usual, God's desire is to bring people who are far from Him into a personal relationship with Him and to bring those who are already close to him even closer. Romans 8:29 reveals to us that God's desired destiny for all of us is to be "conformed to the image of His son." In Acts 27 and 28, we see the plan of God working through that storm to accomplish God's purposes. We should also notice that the process of being refined by suffering and transformed to be more like Christ did not only benefit Paul; it also benefitted every person on that ship, every person on the island of Malta, multitudes in the city of Rome, and every person who has ever been impacted by the scriptures that the Holy Spirit wrote through Paul.

God does not cause every storm that invades our lives, but He always has a purpose in allowing it. In fact, the catalyst of this book came as the result of a prayer about storms. While on vacation one hot and humid July morning, I was having my devotional time in the presence of God, and some of my unanswered questions about the long seasons of adversity that our family has endured began to surface in my prayers. Twenty-seven years after our season of storms began, I was certainly overwhelmed with gratitude to God for miraculously bringing every member of my family through their life-threatening health crises. But I still couldn't comprehend God's purpose for allowing it all to happen.

Then, it was as if the Lord dropped a bombshell of truth on me as I was reading the following verses in 2 Corinthians 1:3-4:

> *Praise be to the God and Father of our Lord Jesus Christ, the Father of compassion and the God of all comfort, who comforts us in all our troubles, so that we can comfort those in any trouble with the comfort we ourselves have received from God.*

The words in those verses that the Holy Spirit emphasized to me that morning were "so that." The Lord spoke into my spirit and said, *Did you ever consider that this was the plan from the beginning? I have comforted and encouraged you through intense seasons of trouble **so that** I could use you to comfort and encourage others who doubt that they can make it through their storms.*

At that moment, I was reminded once again of my God-given dream to write books that God would use to change the trajectory of people's lives and inspire them to walk out their divine destinies in spite of whatever adversity was holding them back. Within minutes of that earth-shaking devotional time, I pulled out my laptop and started writing this book. Many times, in the New Testament, we see the concept of the "fellowship of sufferings." When we go through trials, we tend to have compassion and relate to others who are experiencing those same sufferings. God has used the pathway of suffering in our lives to cultivate a deep compassion and a desire to inspire, encourage, and equip people to *grow* through their trials—not just to *go* through them.

> I understand well the temptation to give up and quit the fight of faith.

I understand well the temptation to give up and quit the fight of faith because I couldn't understand why my family was repeatedly facing life-threatening illnesses. But I am beyond grateful for the Lord's compassion, comfort, and strength as He empowered us to not only survive but to thrive in our darkest days. Our greatest desire is to minister to others who are going through trials and to encourage and comfort them with the same encouragement and comfort that the Lord used to bring us through our storms and into incomprehensible victory! The incredible blessing and favor that we enjoy now would have never happened if we had not partnered with God.

I imagine that before Jesus appeared to the disciples walking on the sea, they were confused, frustrated, and even angry that they had been sent into that storm. But the whole experience enlarged their perception of who Jesus was and built their faith to a much higher level. And that higher level of faith put them in position to be used in greater ways than they ever imagined. I believe that on the other side of their storm, their frustration melted away, and they were filled with gratitude to be called to partner with the Lord to see people's lives transformed.

REFLECTION & APPLICATION

1) What life experiences came to your mind when you read the paragraph that contrasted magic and miracles? Describe a time in your life when your greatest desire was for God to snap His fingers and make your problem disappear.

2) Describe a time in your life when it became obvious to you that God was orchestrating a plan that you were previously unaware of.

3) What is your most significant memory of obediently partnering with God to see His will accomplished in your life? What were the results of that partnership?

4) What purpose has God accomplished in your life as you've partnered with Him?

5) God used Moses to bring people out of bondage. Can you think of a way that God wants to use you to see others set free by God's power?

6) God's plan for David became obvious with his assignment to slay a giant that opposed God's people. David was born to sling that rock and slay Goliath. That airborne stone represented David's acceptance of God's call on his life. We were all born with a divine destiny—a stone to sling. When God created you, He loaded your sling with a stone of specific gifts and talents. But it is up to you to sling that stone. What giant stands in opposition to God's will that needs to fall in your life?

7) A Spiritual Gifts test can be helpful in discovering the unique qualities and giftings that God has crafted into your life. Below you will find information on some well-established and balanced spiritual gifts tests. But there is an important element that you need to understand. A Spiritual Gifts test is a "snapshot" of your giftings. Our lives are not static, we are constantly on a journey. And that means that in different seasons of life, our passion, interests and focus can shift. While there are some elements of your spiritual giftings that will remain steady, other elements of God's design for your life may change over time. Even if you have taken a spiritual gifts assessment in the past, it may be helpful to complete another one to assess your current situation. Here are two good options:
→ C. Peter Wagner, "Discover Your Spiritual Gifts"
→ S.H.A.P.E. Test—Helping You Discover God's Purpose in Life

8) Faith Exercise: Find a smooth stone to carry in your pocket every day as a reminder that you have a "stone to sling"—a divine destiny to fulfill.

SAMPLE PRAYER

Lord, I thank You for the obvious truth that You have a plan for my life, not only in times of blessing but also in times of adversity. I pray that every facet of Your plan will be accomplished in my life as I partner with You by walking in obedience to Your Word and Your will. I also thank You for the amazing blessings and benefits that You desire to provide not only for me but also through me as I cooperate with Your will. I pray that You will use my life to bless others and inspire them to draw closer to You. In Jesus' name, I pray! Amen.

FAITH DECLARATION

Lord, I declare by faith that as I faithfully partner with You in obedience, You will use my life to make a difference in this world as You have done with countless others since the beginning of time. I declare by faith that any giant empowered by Satan to oppose Your plan for my life will be slain as I faithfully use the gifts that You have placed in my hands. I also declare by faith that You will bring me through every storm of adversity that stands between me and Your perfect will. I declare all these things by faith in the name of Jesus!

CHAPTER 13

MORE TIPS FOR THE TEMPEST

Matthew's account of the storm the disciples experienced on the Sea of Galilee was not of the first nor the last storm they encountered. That region was susceptible to atmospheric disturbances that developed quickly. As we have already seen, there are other narratives in the Bible that give detailed accounts of God's people dealing with physical and spiritual storms. The process of navigating adversity is one that can teach us valuable life lessons to equip us for a better future. The narrative of Paul's shipwreck that we covered in the previous chapter contains several powerful and practical principles that can help us in times of trouble.

SEEK GODLY WISDOM

Much time had already been lost, and sailing had already become
dangerous because by now it was after the Fast. So Paul warned
them. "Men, I can see that our voyage is going to be disastrous
and bring great loss to ship and cargo, and to our own lives

also." But the centurion, instead of listening to what Paul said,
followed the advice of the pilot and the owner of the ship.
—Acts 27:9-11

> Often, we seek advice from people who are
> stuck in the same boat that we are in.

In the narrative of Paul's shipwreck recorded in Acts 27, we see that one of the reasons that the shipwreck occurred was that those in charge ignored Paul's warning of impending disaster if they proceeded with their plan. The Bible encourages us to consistently seek for God's wisdom, but this can be even more vital in times of trouble. In good times and bad, it is important that we listen to wise, godly counsel. Often, we seek advice from people who are stuck in the same boat that we are in. The following verses make it clear that we must be diligent to seek godly wisdom from godly people during times of adversity:

→ Proverbs 4:7: "Wisdom is supreme, therefore get wisdom. Though it costs all you have, get understanding."
→ Psalm 37:30: "The mouth of the righteous man utters wisdom, and his tongue speaks what is just."
→ James 1:5: "If any of you lacks wisdom, he should ask God, who gives generously to all without finding fault, and it will be given to him."

While it is true that the Bible encourages us to listen to godly counsel from godly people, we must not forget that the ultimate source of godly wisdom is the Lord Himself. As we have covered earlier in the book, we must make prayer a priority. Oftentimes, we need a specific word from the Lord to guide us through situations. James 1:5 is a favorite verse for many people. I rarely live a single day that I don't quote it as a part of my prayer life. But a lot of people fail to realize that this verse is not just a general petition for wisdom. It was written in the specific context of facing trials, trouble, and temptations of all kinds. This is yet another indication of the extreme value of seeking God's wisdom in times of adversity.

The narrative of Paul's shipwreck in Acts 27:23-25 contains another example of this principle:

> "Last night an angel of the God to whom I belong and whom I serve stood beside me and said, 'Do not be afraid, Paul. You must stand trial before Caesar, and God has graciously given you the lives of all who sail with you.' So keep up your courage, men, for I have faith in God that it will happen just as he told me."

As Paul spent time in prayer during his storm, God gave him a specific word to encourage and guide him. That word from the Lord not only affected Paul but served as much-needed encouragement for all those in the storm with Paul.

As Paul spent time in prayer during his storm, God gave him a specific word to encourage and guide him.

REINFORCE YOUR LIFE

*The ship was caught by the storm and could not head into the
wind, so we gave way to it and were driven along. As we passed
to the lee of a small island called Cauda, we were hardly able
to make the lifeboat secure, so the men hoisted it aboard. Then
they passed ropes under the ship itself to hold it together....*
—Acts 27:15-17

An interesting part of this story involves an ancient mariner's technique called frapping. No, this has nothing to do with Frappuccino blended iced coffee drinks! This technique was used particularly in extremely rough and stormy seas. When the crew sensed that their vessel was in danger of breaking up due to the pounding of the waves, they would pass strong ropes under the hull of the ship and secure them tightly in order to reinforce the structure of the vessel. We all face times when we need help, and the willingness to reach out in our time of need is a significant predictor of survival. So how do we get reinforcements when life's winds and waves are pounding against us?

First, as we just saw in the life of Paul, we get reinforcement through our relationship with God. A prayerful life is a powerful life, and a prayerless life is a powerless life. We gain strength as we invest significant time in the presence of God. As we consistently spend time in worship and prayer, the Holy Spirit inhabits our lives in increasing measures. To build our relationship with God requires some of the same elements that it takes to build any other relationship. We must spend time in focused communication and fellowship with the Lord. The more time we invest in His presence, the more sensitive we become to His voice as He speaks into our lives. We also become more keenly aware of His presence as we go about our daily routines.

Now it's time for an unexpected question. Have you ever gotten a love letter from someone that you really liked? I hope the answer is yes. Assuming that you have gotten at least one love note, I have some follow-up questions to ask. Did you take the time to read the letter? Did you read the letter more than once in an attempt to not only absorb the content but also to try to read between the lines for anything below the surface of the words? I have used this question many times through the years as an illustration, and every time, the majority of the crowd raised their hand to indicate that they had not only read a love letter once—but over and over again to glean any hint of how the letter's author felt about them.

God's Word is His love letter to us! In it, He expresses how much He loves us and wants to empower us to fulfill the destiny for which we were created. Unfortunately, many people who believe in God and have trusted in Christ as their Savior invest very little time reading God's love letter. The Bible is a primary way that God speaks to us. If we want to reinforce our lives by seeking a closer relationship with God, we must consistently spend time reading and studying God's Word. As we covered in earlier chapters, we desperately need a word from God to give us direction in life.

A second way that we can reinforce our lives is by staying connected in relationships with fellow believers. As we already covered, it is imperative that we avoid isolation by cultivating healthy relationships with others. You may recall from earlier chapters that Jesus Himself set this example for us in the garden of Gethsemane by staying connected to His disciples in a very intense time of struggle. We should never be timid about calling in reinforcements. The Bible is consistent in its encouragement to build and maintain healthy fellowship and communion with other followers of Christ.

> We should never be timid about
> calling in reinforcements.

REORDER YOUR PRIORITIES

*We took such a violent battering from the storm that the next
day they began to throw the cargo overboard. On the third day,
they threw the ship's tackle overboard with their own hands.*
—Acts 27:18-19

The main motivation for the ship's captain and crew to set sail in
spite of the impending storm was financial. They were willing to take
the risk because of the monetary rewards of delivering the ship's cargo
to its intended destination. But they soon had a major shift in their
priorities. Isn't it amazing how a storm in life can change our perception of what really matters? Under normal circumstances, there is
no way that the crew would have thrown their cargo overboard. But
the storm recalibrated their values. What good would it do to try to
preserve a big "payday" if they were dead at the bottom of the sea?

It is easy for us to get distracted by priorities that are out of alignment with God's plan. One of the sources of dysfunction in our lives
appears when we overvalue things that are not important and under-
value the things that really matter. Early in our decades-long season
of life-threatening storms, I was challenged to view every moment
through the lens of what really matters. Within a year of Colton's
birth, I started collecting hourglasses. You may be thinking, *What
in the world does that have to do with anything?* I'm glad you asked.

As I noticed an hourglass in a store that became the first one in my collection, it was as if the Lord spoke a profound word into my heart. No matter what I choose to do with my time—the sand is always running. I can choose to waste the precious moments of life focusing on things that are worthless—or I can choose to focus my attention on the things that really matter. That powerful thought continually reminds me of how blessed I am to be able to spend time with my wife and children, especially after coming so close to losing all of them so many times.

I don't believe that there is another generation in human history that has battled with constant distraction the way we do. The modern technology that has *put the world at our fingertips* has also made focused thought something that we literally have to fight for. The ability to sit in quietness and think has almost become a thing of the past for most people whose attention is constantly being arrested by bells, beeps, and notifications of all kinds from their smartphones and other devices.

Don't wait for the next storm to strike. Take time now to get alone with God and ask for His help to reorder your priorities in alignment with your divine destiny. The sailors aboard the ship with Paul rearranged their priorities based on what really mattered. They lightened their load by getting rid of extra baggage that was weighing the ship down and threatening their survival. We all need to do the same thing. Seek the Lord's guidance regarding distractions in your life that need to be thrown overboard so that you will be free to focus on the things that really matter.

STAY ANCHORED

Acts 27:29 describes what the crew did next: "Fearing that we would be dashed against the rocks, they dropped four anchors from the stern and prayed for daylight." Anchors are important regardless of whether the waters are rough or smooth. I am not much of a fisherman, but I have been fishing a few times on a river or a lake. I remember going fishing on a river with my dad when I was a kid. One reason that memory stands out to me is that even though the river current was almost undetectable, I was surprised when I looked up and noticed that we had drifted a long way downstream.

Anchors are designed to hold a vessel in the proper location and keep it from drifting out of position. *Drift* is not only a problem in sailing—it is a problem in life! How many times in life have you suddenly become aware that you have drifted off course? There are so many influences in this world that are constantly trying to move us in the wrong direction. We need anchors to keep us in position.

Without an anchor, the storms of life can cause us to drift out of position and move away from God's destiny for our lives. The Greek word for "anchor" in the verse above is used only four times in the New Testament. One of those is found in Hebrews 6:19-20:

> *We have this hope as an anchor for the soul, firm and secure. It enters the inner sanctuary behind the curtain, where Jesus, who went before us, has entered on our behalf. . . .*

The imagery of verse 19 essentially declares that our hope in Christ is literally anchored into the very presence of God. How did our anchor get into that position? Verse 20 states that the reason is because Jesus went before us and entered into the presence of God on our behalf. Keeping a proper focus on our relationship with Christ cultivates hope that anchors us in a healthy position spiritually.

As is so often the case, there are encouraging treasures of truth beneath the surface in these verses. The phrase in verse 20 that states that Jesus "went before us" comes from a single Greek word *prodromos*, which literally means "a forerunner" or "one who goes before." In those days, that Greek word was also used to refer to a small boat with a specific purpose. Either in times of storm or in cases where a ship lacked the ability to safely navigate a dangerous passage into a harbor, the ship's anchor would be dropped into a smaller boat referred to as the forerunner. The forerunner would then carry the ship's anchor through the treacherous passage until it could safely and securely drop the anchor into the exact location of the ship's final destination in the safety of the harbor. The ship would then simply draw itself through the danger zone by pulling itself towards the anchor until it safely reached its destination.

These images illustrate the fact that, on our own, we do not have the ability to navigate safely through the perilous waters of life. However, because of what the Lord has done for us, our hope in Christ has anchored our soul into the very presence of God. As long as we maintain our connection with the Lord, we can be safely drawn through the storms we face and arrive at God's intended destiny for our lives.

> As long as we maintain our connection with the Lord, we can be safely drawn through the storms we face and arrive at God's intended destiny for our lives.

PREPARE BEFORE THE STORM

Immediately Jesus made the disciples get into the boat and go on ahead of him to the other side, while he dismissed the crowd.

After he had dismissed them, he went up on a mountainside by himself to pray. When the evening came, he was there alone, but the boat was already a considerable distance from land, buffeted by the waves because the wind was against it.
—Matthew 14:22-24

To glean the final *tip for the tempest*, we will go back to the initial verses of the storm we have highlighted throughout the book. As we have discovered, the disciples had no idea that a storm was coming, but I believe that Jesus did. He knew how the faith of the disciples would be built up to a new level because of what they were about to experience. Throughout the gospels, we see evidence that Jesus displayed a faithful commitment to consistently withdraw from the crowds to spend significant amounts of time in prayer and solitude in the presence of God the Father.

It is enlightening to recognize that Jesus was always ready when significant events occurred because He had been praying and preparing in advance. We see that same pattern emerge in this story. Walking on stormy seas was not something that Jesus had ever done before, but He knew the plan that God had in mind, so He spent time in prayerful preparation. We have seen a large number of hurricane-force storms make landfall and cause extensive damage in the past several years. You have probably seen newscasts from the target zones that show highways backed up with traffic for miles as people attempt to evacuate the area.

On-the-scene reporters often interview people who are boarding up their doors and windows or filling up sandbags to form flood barriers. It makes perfect sense to us in the case of an actual physical storm that all those precautions need to be completed before the storm hits.

It would be foolish to wait until the storm is bearing down on us to start making things ready. The same is true for unexpected times of crisis. Even though we can't always see them approaching, we know from experience that tough seasons will come. Making ourselves ready before the storm hits is a key to survival.

One of the main purposes of this book is to encourage people who are experiencing times of crisis and equip them with foundational biblical principles to help them come through their storms stronger than ever. Proactively engaging the principles highlighted in this book will strengthen and prepare you to persevere through any adversity that comes your way. My family would likely not have survived and would certainly not have thrived through our decades-long season of adversity if we had not been strengthened and prepared by the eternal principles of God's Word. Our sincere prayer is that the comfort that we have received from the Lord (2 Corinthians 1:3-4) and the lessons that we have learned in our seasons of adversity will be used by God as valuable resources to help people grow through their times of trouble and inhabit the promised land of their divine destiny.

REFLECTION & APPLICATION

1) Describe a time when you were certain that you had received wisdom from God to guide your pathway. Did you embrace that wisdom or ignore it? What lesson can you learn from that experience to help you in the future?

2) Based on the content of this chapter, what decisions can you make and what actions can you take to "reinforce your life"?

3) What do you believe that the Lord is revealing to you about things in your life that you need to cast overboard to reorder your priorities and lighten your load?

4) What are you doing to maintain your "connection" to your hope in Christ? An anchor only works when the chain continues to keep it connected to the ship. Jesus has gone before you and dropped your anchor in your final destination. Keep that connection strong, and it will pull you through your storms.

SAMPLE PRAYER

Lord, I thank You for Your generous offer and provision of the godly wisdom that I need. I ask in faith, according to Your Word in James 1:5, that You will fill me with Your wisdom and help me to follow the pathway of Your perfect will for my life. Thank You for helping me reinforce my life through an intimate, healthy relationship with You and with my brothers and sisters in Christ that You have placed in my life. Please reveal to me anything that is weighing me down that needs to be thrown overboard so that I can focus more fully on Your destiny for me. I pray that You will help me to stay anchored in my faith, hope, and trust in You so that I can be prepared for the future. I pray these things in the mighty name of Jesus. Amen.

FAITH DECLARATION

Lord, I declare by faith that I receive a steady flow of Your wisdom to guide my life. I declare that my life will be reinforced to a level of strength that I have never attained as I act on Your Word. I declare that I will be willing to cast overboard the things You reveal to me that need to go, and I will focus on maintaining a strong connection with You through my hope in Christ which is already anchored in my divine destiny in Your presence. I declare all these things by faith in Christ!

CHAPTER 14

THE OTHER SIDE: WHEN YOU HAVE CROSSED OVER

"When they had crossed over, they landed at Gennesaret."
—Matthew 14:34

Until Jesus appeared atop the waves, the disciples likely had serious doubts that they would ever see the other side of the lake. Sound familiar? Have you ever gone through a trial so daunting that you didn't think you would ever make it through to the other side? As you already know, our family has been in that place repeatedly. Many times in prayer, I've told the Lord that I did not think that we could stand another crisis. We have seen times when we were so weary of the fight that giving up seemed like a viable option. But when you stick it out, stay faithful, and navigate through the storm, one thing that you will find on the other side is an intense feeling of gratitude to God for bringing you through and a great sense of relief that you didn't give up. On the other side, you realize all the blessings of the Lord that you would have forfeited if you had listened to your emotions and quit the struggle.

On the other side, you realize all the blessings of the Lord that you would have forfeited if you had listened to your emotions and quit the struggle.

TAKE THE RIGHT FORK

In earlier chapters, I mentioned times when I got stuck in my questions and was very close to giving up as a result of the continual attacks that came against my family. I explained earlier that after we go through all of the emotional turmoil and all of the unanswered questions, we generally find ourselves at a *fork in the road.* One fork takes us down a *pathway of paralysis.* We are tempted to stop moving forward and just give up. Our reasoning is that if we can't understand what is happening, we should just forget the whole thing. At times when we are overwhelmed with attacks from all sides, we have a tendency to stop trusting God and start interrogating him.

The other choice, the *right fork,* takes us on a different pathway. The right (correct) fork takes us on a *pathway of progress.* We choose to move forward in spite of our unanswered questions. We still don't like the situation, and we still don't understand it, but we look over the whole scope of our life and realize that we have come too far and seen too much to turn back now. Our attitude is one that says, *I don't like this situation, and I would change it if I could, but I cannot ignore all the times in the past that God has worked in my life. I know too much to walk away from the Lord. So, my only reasonable choice is to basically say, "Lord, I don't understand this, but I am going to keep moving forward.*

*When I don't understand—**I'll still stand!** I am going to continue to trust You in this crisis. I choose to believe that You didn't just bring me to it; You will bring me through it.*

Looking back now, I still don't like all the suffering that my family has endured, but I am so grateful that I did not take the wrong fork. I am so glad that I did not give up on God simply because I was angry at Him for allowing our trials. If I had walked away, my family would not be in the amazingly healthy place that we are in today. If I had walked away from God, there is no telling how far my rage would have taken me. I most certainly would have become a very different person, and that person's influence in the lives of my children could have been very destructive. If I had taken the wrong path, I might have unintentionally sacrificed my children on the altar of my anger. I am so grateful that instead of walking away from God because of my unanswered questions, I chose to walk with Him in spite of them. That choice has led us to a place of incredible blessing and favor that fills me with gratitude every day!

THE TESTIMONY AFTER THE TEST

Now might be a good time to give you the latest updates on how our family is doing. In spite of his multiple heart defects, six open-heart surgeries, and numerous other heart-related procedures: Colton is living a very full life! He just turned thirty years old and has been living on his own and very successfully *adulting* for several years. He is strong, healthy, and even athletic! He has grown into a wonderful young man, and I am extremely proud to be his father. He loves the Lord, He loves people, and He is very compassionate. He has many friends, a great attitude, and a great work ethic. His future is bright because of the way He has responded to all the suffering He has faced.

Although it took years for Nancy to recover from her illness, she made slow but steady progress for about ten years. At that point, she made a courageous decision to do everything in her power to take back her health. She began to steadily ramp-up her physical exercise routines, and within eighteen months, she had lost over one hundred pounds! Twelve years after she almost died from her disease, she was in the best shape of her adult life. Not only that, but her body responded well to the new fitness regimen, and within a few months, her doctors were able to take her off almost all the medications that she had been taking as a result of the disease. To this day, she is maintaining a healthy level of fitness.

Anna Grace continues to thrive and develop into the person that God designed her to be, in spite of all the obstacles that she has had to overcome. She is an amazing young lady! She loves the Lord, and she loves people. She is compassionate and wants to invest her life in helping others and making a positive difference in the world. That little miracle baby that we were told might not ever walk, talk, or live a normal life has completed three years of college and is one of the most beloved employees at her job. As of this writing, she is now engaged to be married and has a very bright future.

My suffering through most of our decades-long season of storms was based on watching the people I love most in this world face death repeatedly. Even though I didn't have any serious health issues until recently, I experienced the pain and feelings of helplessness that accompany watching the people we love suffer terribly. My health challenges didn't begin until my near-fatal heart attack in November of 2021 and my diagnosis of two brain aneurysms in January of 2022. But the Lord has been very gracious and helped me to *beat the odds*, just like He did for the rest of my family.

GREATER THINGS ARE WAITING ON THE OTHER SIDE

As we have seen, one of the most well-known stories in all of the Bible precedes this entire narrative of the storm. Before the disciples got into the boat to cross over to the other side of the lake, they had spent the entire day with Jesus as He taught the multitudes and, eventually, multiplied the fish and loaves to feed a massive gathering of over five thousand men. It is unlikely that the crowd consisted solely of men, and if women and children were present, the crowd size could have been closer to twenty thousand. That account mentions that Jesus had compassion on the people and performed some healings, but the main focus is on the feeding of the five thousand.

So, what happened on the other side of their storm?

And when the men of that place recognized Jesus, they sent word to all the surrounding country. People brought all their sick to him and begged him to let the sick just touch the edge of his cloak, and all who touched it were healed. —Matthew 14:35-36

In their personal lives, their faith was bolstered, and their understanding of who Jesus really was increased. And once they had crossed over to the other side, there were other results that began to materialize. The above verses indicate that once people realized that Jesus was there, they brought all their sick to Him, and every single one of them was healed! One of the things that we observe in this passage is that once the disciples made it through the storm, the other side became a place of greater impact.

Once the disciples made it through
the storm, the other side became
a place of greater impact.

The main focus of the verses preceding the storm was the miracle of feeding the multitudes. The main focus of the verses after the storm was the miracle of healing the multitudes. What makes the greater impact—eating a fish sandwich or getting healed from a deadly disease? *The other side* that Jesus wants to lead us to—is a place of greater effectiveness and greater impact! The principles of God's Word, as well as my own life experience, have taught me that the other side of the storm has the potential to be a place of "greater things." Greater faith, greater peace, greater joy, and greater impact are all waiting for you on the other side of your storm.

These verses have become a defining truth in our family:

Praise be to the God and Father of our Lord Jesus Christ, the Father of compassion and the God of all comfort, who comforts us in all our troubles, so that we can comfort those in any trouble with the comfort we ourselves receive from God. —2 Corinthians 1:3-4

There is a principle that we have often witnessed in the lives of God's people. As we have already mentioned, if we choose to respond correctly to our storms, *God can transform the pain of misery into the power of ministry!* There are two often-overlooked words in verse 4 above that are a key to understanding what the Lord is saying to us through that verse. God comforts us in all our troubles "SO THAT" we can comfort others that are going through tough times. We are to comfort them "with the comfort that we ourselves receive from God."

TELL YOUR STORY

There are many verses in the Scriptures that encourage us to tell our story. One such instance is found in Acts 1:8: "But you will receive power when the Holy Spirit comes on you, and you will be my witnesses in Jerusalem, and in all Judea and Samaria, and to the ends of the earth." Different streams of Christianity tend to approach this verse from different angles. But in its most basic form, the verse states that the Holy Spirit will empower us to be a witness for Christ. Part of the confusion seems to be centered around the word "witness." Many times people read that word in this verse and seem to confuse it with the word "preach." Somewhere along the way, people have gotten the idea that being a witness is the same thing as preaching about Jesus.

We have totally missed the simplicity of our instructions. Every believer is called to be a witness, not a preacher. It would be helpful at this point to recall what a witness actually does. When I was a little boy, my mom loved to watch Perry Mason on TV. I didn't care for the show back then, but I did glean some helpful information from watching what goes on in a courtroom setting.

In the courtroom, the job of a witness is not complicated at all. The witness is there to simply tell what they have seen or what they have heard. In essence, they *tell their story* as it relates to the matter before the court. That is what we are called to do. We are called to tell what we have seen and what we have heard—what we have seen God do in our life and what we have heard Him speak into our life. We are called *to tell our story as a witness to others.* That should cause far less anxiety than thinking we need to be prepared to preach or debate the Scriptures. No one can tell your story as well as you can because no one else has lived it. Our testimony is a customized introduction that can lead into the opportunity to share the simple gospel of Christ.

Tell your story!

Has your life ever been impacted in a positive way by hearing someone else's story? Most likely, the answer is yes. Aren't you glad that person told their story? If they had kept silent, the impact they made on you would never have happened. *An untold story makes no impact.*

> # An untold story makes no impact.

You never know what God could do if you would allow Him to empower you to be a witness that shares the testimony of how the Lord has helped you to make it through your toughest days.

I don't like that my children have suffered, but that experience has led to hundreds of opportunities through the years for Nancy and me to minister to families who were facing trials with the health of their children. I may not be an expert at everything in life, but I know how to communicate hope to parents whose world has just fallen apart because of a devasting diagnosis.

No one can tell our story as well as we can. And no one can tell your story as well as you can. When you make it through your storm, one of the results will be that you will have the opportunity to make a huge difference in the lives of other people who are struggling with a similar situation. You will have true and genuine compassion for them because of what you have experienced. And you will have real-life wisdom about how to navigate those rough seas because you have been there and done that. You may also find that once your story becomes known, people will seek you out to ask how you were able to not only survive but actually thrive in spite of your circumstances. In those moments, 2 Corinthians 1:3-4 will become an indelible imprint in your *understanding of your destiny* in God's kingdom.

DISCOVERING A DIVINE DESTINY

Speaking of destiny, years ago, as I was spending time with the Lord one morning, I was reading Psalm 139. I was writing in my journal some thoughts on the verses in that chapter when I noticed something in verse 16: "Your eyes saw my unformed body, all the days ordained for me were written in your book before one of them came to be." In this passage about the miraculous way in which God creates each new human life in the womb, this verse goes beyond the description of creation and speaks of destiny.

Every single person is born with a destiny in the plan of God. "All the days ordained for me were written in your book before one of them came to be." This indicates that God has a vision for our lives. He has a pathway that He has designed for us to walk and a purpose that He has destined us to fulfill. While this verse clearly points to divine destiny in our lives, it does not indicate that our destiny is guaranteed.

My understanding of this verse is that God has created each one of us with a divine destiny to fulfill. And that vision is recorded in heaven. But, as we see in other places in the Scriptures, free will has a part to play. God does not impose His plan on our lives; He allows us to choose whether or not we will follow His plan. If we choose to follow His plan, then we will have the amazing privilege of living life with a keen sense of divine purpose and guidance. If we choose not to follow God's plan, then, unfortunately, we will be spending the precious life we have been given doing something other than what we were created to accomplish.

Weird question: Have you ever driven a nail using something other than a hammer? I personally have used a shoe, a brick, the handle of a screwdriver, the side of a pair of pliers, and probably some other stuff to drive a nail when a hammer wasn't handy. All those items eventually got the job done, but they were nowhere nearly as effective as a hammer would have been. Why? Because a hammer was designed to drive nails. Isn't it amazing how much easier a task can be when we use the right tools for the right job?

We all have a choice of how we want to spend our life. But doesn't it make sense that we should try to discover the divine purpose for which we were designed, and spend our lifetime living out that destiny? You are the right tool for the right job. God has designed you for a specific purpose, and that is why Satan works so hard to kill, steal, and destroy our God-given dreams. Ephesians 2:10, "For we are God's workmanship, created in Christ Jesus to do good works, which God prepared in advance for us to do" is yet another verse among many that confirms the principles of this chapter.

God created you with a divine destiny to do good and make a difference. The Greek word for "workmanship" in this verse is a root of the English word "poem." Why is that significant? Because a poem is not just a bunch of unrelated words scribbled on paper. A poem has a well-thought-out structure, cadence, rhythm, and rhyme. Many scholars indicate that workmanship in this verse implies a "masterpiece of craftsmanship." This is what God's Word says about you! The enemy of your soul, your own mind and the voices of other people may speak the exact opposite about you from what God says. Silence those voices and focus on God's prophetic declarations of your divine destiny and God-given dreams.

In this context, I have come to accept that God's plan for our family to make a great impact and inspire people to keep moving forward in spite of their storms required us to navigate treacherous seas to prepare us for that mission. That is a perception that is almost impossible to recognize while you are still in the middle of your crisis, but if you keep your trust in the Lord, it may very well become obvious to you down the road.

I encourage you to take a higher view of your situation and realize that when the Lord brings you through your crisis, you may become the lifeline that someone else needs to keep them from giving up. Everything about the other side of the storm is greater. That is one reason Satan tries so desperately to defeat us in the storm. He works tirelessly to keep us distracted and discouraged in an attempt to increase the chances that we might give up. He does all of this because he actually dreads the powerful impact we could make . . . on the other side!

If we give in to discouragement and give up, that decision will not only be detrimental to us—it will also damage the lives of all the people that God intended for us to encourage and comfort. Don't get distracted. Don't get discouraged. Keep putting one foot in front of the other, and you will keep moving forward. Don't Give Up! You can make it through your storm all the way to the other side—and greater things are waiting for you there!

REFLECTION & APPLICATION

1) Describe a time when you felt like you were standing at a fork in the road, and you were confused about which way to go.

2) What life lessons have you learned from your choices at the fork in the road?

3) How can you engage the principles of this chapter to become the witness that God wants to use to spread your story of how He has worked in your life?

4) How do the desires of your heart line up with God's Word to indicate the pathway of your divine destiny? What is your God-given dream?

SAMPLE PRAYER

Lord, I pray for Your guidance in the days when I find myself at a fork in the road. Help me to always make my choices based on the wisdom of Your Word and not the emotions of the moment. I thank You for all the principles in Your Word that declare that You have specifically designed my life to accomplish great things for You. Help me to reject the voices that contradict what Your Word declares about my life and the potential that You have built into me. I ask that You continue to speak into my life and lead me in the pathway of my divine destiny and God-given dreams. I pray all these things in the mighty name of Jesus! Amen.

FAITH DECLARATION

Lord, I declare by faith that I will make it safely through every storm as You lead, guide, and protect me in the process. I declare that I will prayerfully choose the right fork in the road every time I am faced with a choice. I also declare that I will faithfully pursue the destiny for which I was created and not allow the enemy to stop me from moving forward. I declare that all of these choices will not only positively impact my life but also the lives of all the people that You intend for me to reach with my testimony of Your goodness. I declare all of these things by faith in the name of Jesus.

GREG DAVIS

Presents

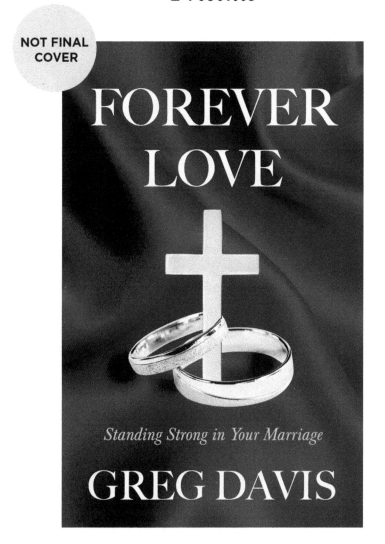

NOT FINAL
COVER

FOREVER LOVE

Standing Strong in Your Marriage

GREG DAVIS

Available Spring 2023